Missouri

BY THEME

DAY TRIPS

Brian Blair

Adventure Publications
Cambridge, Minnesota

Safety Note Missouri is home to a variety of potentially dangerous animals, including venomous snakes, as well as natural hazards, such as temperature extremes, sudden flash floods, and cliffs and dropoffs. Always heed posted safety warnings, take common-sense safety precautions, and remain aware of your surroundings. You're responsible for your own safety.

Editors: Brett Ortler, Ritchey Halphen, and Kate Johnson
Cover and book design by Jonathan Norberg

Front cover photo: Alley Mill National Park, Eminence, MO: **K Welschmeyer/shutterstock.com;** map: **Globe Turner/shutterstock.com**
Back cover photo: Elephant Rocks State Park, MO: **Fredlyfish4/shutterstock.com**

Photos by **Brian Blair** except as follows:
Courtesy of the Smithsonian: 134 (Hadrosaur)

Photos used under license from Shutterstock.com:
Avik: 115; **Ben Bondurant:** 120; **Brandon B:** 119; **Brett Godfrey:** 72; **Brian Ridge:** 41; **Callie Wyrsch:** 92; **Cheri Alguire:** 20; **Cholpan:** 128 (top); **CLP Media:** 26; **Comet Design:** 127 (flag); eurobanks: 126; **Everett Collection:** 34; **Filip Bjorkman:** 127 (map); **Ganeshkumar Durai:** 82; **Homeschoolmomshop:** 65; IrinaK: 133 (top); ivan_kislitsin: 122; **Jeff Zarinelli:** 55; **Jon Kraft:** 132 (top); **Karen Bahr:** 111; LanaG: 14, 4, 116; **Laurens Hoddenbagh:** 58; **Leonard Jerry Horsford:** 25; **Malachi Ives:** 63; **Marco Fine:** 130 (galena); marekuliasz: 4; **Matej Kastelic:** 124; **M.Curtis:** 28; **Mia2you:** 9; **Mikael Damkier:** 81; **NSC Photography:** 23, 133 (bottom); **Nick Tre. Smith:** 108; **Paul Michael Hughes:** 135; **Rabbitti:** 129 (bottom); **Rob Neville Photos:** 85, 90; RozenskiP: 66; **Saran Jantraurai:** 132 (bottom); **Sergey Goruppa:** 129 (top); **Simun Ascic:** 130 (bottom); **Spandau_ Goulet:** 13; **Tau5:** 131 (bottom); **Tinnaporn Sathapornnanont:** 57; **TommyBrison:** 48; **Virunja:** 128 (bottom); **Wirestock Creators:** 52; **Zack Frank:** 102

This image is licensed under the Attribution 2.0 Generic (CC BY 2.0) license, which is available at https://creativecommons.org/licenses/by/2.0/: **James St. John:** 131 (top), ["Synbathocrinus fossil crinoid (Burlington Limestone, Mississippian; Missouri, USA) 1" (unaltered)], original photo via: https://www.flickr.com/photos/jsjgeology/17383990962

This image is licensed under the CC0 1.0 Universal (CC0 1.0) Public Domain Dedication license, which is available at https://creativecommons.org/publicdomain/zero/1.0/: **Astynax:** 130 (mozarkite)

10 9 8 7 6 5 4 3 2 1

Missouri Day Trips by Theme
Copyright © 2021 by Brian Blair
Published by Adventure Publications
An imprint of AdventureKEEN
310 Garfield Street South
Cambridge, Minnesota 55008
(800) 678-7006
www.adventurepublications.net
All rights reserved
Printed in the United States of America
ISBN 978-1-59193-953-5 (pbk.); ISBN 978-1-59193-954-2 (ebook)

Disclaimer Please note that travel information changes under the impact of many factors that influence the travel industry. We therefore suggest that you call ahead for confirmation when making your travel plans. Every effort has been made to ensure the accuracy of information throughout this book, and the contents of this publication are believed to be correct at the time of printing. Nevertheless, the publishers cannot accept responsibility for errors or omissions, for changes in details given in this guide, or for the consequences of any reliance on the information provided by the same. Assessments of attractions and so forth are based upon the author's own experiences; therefore, descriptions given in this guide necessarily contain an element of subjective opinion, which may not reflect the publisher's opinion or dictate a reader's own experience on another occasion.

For the latest information about destinations in this book that have been affected by the coronavirus, please check the phone numbers and websites in the trip profiles. For news and updates about the coronavirus in Missouri, see health.mo.gov.

Table of Contents

Dedication

For my Mom, who showed me how beautiful Missouri can be.

Katy Trail at Rocheport

Acknowledgments

A huge thank-you to the Missouri Division of State Parks and the many, many professional park stewards, naturalists, tour guides, and welcome center staff who took time out of their busy jobs to tell me everything they knew and loved about Missouri. Thanks to the friendly folks I met in campgrounds and diners across the state who turned me on to hidden gems and gladly shared their regional expertise. Another massive thank-you to family and friends who let my family park our old rattletrap RV in their driveways when we needed to take a breather. And, of course, a thank-you to my wife and daughter for sharing these months on the road with me.

Note: For readers who might be curious about a theme but not sure if they're ready to commit to a full day trip, you won't find the trips ordered alphabetically within theme sections. Rather, I've arranged each section so that the first few entries contain what I recommend as some of the best experiences in each category. This way, trying something new is sure to be a risk worth taking, and maybe you'll even find a new favorite theme along the way!

Lily Pad Room in Onondaga Cave, National Landmark

THE ROLLING HILLS and high, rocky mountains of the Show-Me State are only half the story. Thanks to vast areas of karst geology covering over half the state, Missouri has another nickname, The Cave State. With more than 6,000 caves—and more discovered each year—you'll have no trouble finding a place to get down underground no matter where you are.

CAVES

1 Round Spring Cave

13209 Round Spring Campground Road, Eminence, MO 65466;
National Park Service 573-858-3297
nps.gov/ozar/planyourvisit/round-spring-and-round-spring-cave.htm

Round Spring Cave in the Ozark National Scenic Riverways is one of the most pristine wild caves open to the public in Missouri. Once you've entered beyond the iron gate, you'll feel as if you've truly taken a step back in time, as there are no floodlights or laser light shows like in so many modern cave tours. It's just you, your lantern, and the spectacular formations on display as you experience the cave in much the same way that early explorers did a hundred years ago. Keep an eye out for rare salamanders (usually most visible during the early-morning tour), and marvel at the deep cuts left in the mud by the claws of massive cave bears who hibernated here thousands of years ago.

2 Jacob's Cave

23114 State Highway TT, Versailles, MO 65084; 573-378-4374
jacobscave.com

The largest cave in the Lake of the Ozarks region, Jacob's Cave offers a magnificent variety of beautiful formations. One of Missouri's few fully accessible caves, it has no slippery stairs, plus it has a fully paved walking path for tours. This is a living cave, with dripping stalactites, soda straws, flowing onyx, and more, so that visitors can truly get a view of the natural forces that made these formations and is still sculpting them today. Because this is a locally owned cave, there is still an intimate, friendly aspect to the tours that can sometimes get lost in the more commercialized show caves. Three times a year, Jacob's Cave also hosts thousands of visitors at a swap meet held in their nearby campground, featuring animals and goods from all over the Ozarks. Check the website for details.

Meramec Caverns, Sullivan

Caves

3 Fantastic Caverns

4872 N. Farm Road 125, Springfield, MO 65803; 417-833-2010
fantasticcaverns.com

Missouri's only ride-through cave, Fantastic Caverns utilizes a fleet of propane-powered trams to roll you through a cave that truly lives up to its name. Anyone and everyone, regardless of physical ability, can enjoy the Hall of Giants, draperies, and cavern theater as you ride comfortably across the ancient riverbed that originally formed the cave. Fun facts include that this cave was first explored in the 1800s by 12 members of the Springfield Women's Athletic Club and that the cave was first discovered by a dog. The current owners of the cave continue to honor this four-legged pioneer by allowing well-behaved pooches to accompany their families on the tour—a rarity you won't find elsewhere. This is truly a cave tour for the whole family.

4 Onondaga Cave & Cathedral Cave

Onondaga Cave State Park, 7556 Highway H, Leasburg, MO 65535; 573-245-6576
mostateparks.com/park/onondaga-cave-state-park

Two caves in one trip! Missouri State Parks manages both caves in this 1,300-acre state park full of rolling hills and clear streams. Onondaga Cave offers a more conventional cave tour, with well-lit formations and paved walkways that showcase the cave's still-active river system and striking formations. Cathedral Cave is an option for those seeking a longer tour and more of the wild-cave experience. Tours lit only by lantern require a bit of a hike and a little more planning, as they're available only on weekends to minimize impact on cave life. Both caves are open only from late spring until October, so make sure to check the website or call ahead to make sure a time is available for your visit.

5 Mark Twain Cave & Cameron Cave

300 Cave Hollow Road, Hannibal, MO 63401; 573-221-1656
marktwaincave.com

Two very different tours, one with a connection to one of America's most celebrated writers. Mark Twain Cave is a labyrinth of tunnels

10

that inspired a young Samuel Clemens and later featured prominently in *The Adventures of Tom Sawyer*. A unique cave experience with numerous interconnected tunnels and stark, sheer walls gives the impression of a catacomb hewn from stone. Actors in full costume portray characters from *Tom Sawyer,* and tours include stops where events from the book "really" happened. Cameron Cave, discovered in 1925, has all the beautiful formations you expect and is treated like a typical wild cave, offering only flashlight-illuminated tours. Mark Twain Cave is open year-round, while Cameron Cave is open only from Memorial Day through Labor Day to help protect its native bat population.

6 Marvel Cave

Silver Dollar City, 399 Silver Dollar City Parkway, Branson, MO 65616; 800-888-7277
silverdollarcity.com/theme-park/attractions/rides/marvel-cave

Holding the distinction of Missouri's deepest cave, Marvel Cave also has a notably massive entrance and an extensively documented history that features prominently during tours. Two tours are offered: a conventional tour of up to 60 visitors and a lantern tour (for an additional fee) limited to a more intimate 20-person group; the latter also features guides in period 1880s costumes. With Marvel being such a deep cave, both tours are mostly spent climbing or descending stairs and so may not be appropriate for those with mobility or health concerns. One additional caveat: All Marvel Cave tours require purchase of a one-day admission to the entire theme park. This does make Marvel Cave one of the most expensive cave experiences in Missouri—but also one that offers a full day of entertainment.

7 Meramec Caverns

1135 Highway W, Sullivan, MO 63080; 573-468-2283
americascave.com

The quintessential show cave, Meramec Caverns has been continually developed as an entertainment destination for nearly 100 years. Though magnificent geology is the main attraction, a P. T. Barnum level of showmanship is also on display in the Jesse James mannequins still hiding out along the tour and in the extensive, colorful lighting that brings a carnival atmosphere to the depths. Toward the end of the tour, there's even a patriotic light show featuring waving flags and a soaring rendition of "America the Beautiful" that plays out against one of the cave's many onyx curtains. Once your tour has ended, pick up some souvenirs in the massive gift shop, rent a canoe, ride a riverboat, or even go on a zipline adventure. Looking for a cave with more razzmatazz? Then follow the endless billboards to this natural spectacle.

8 Stark Caverns

125 Cave Drive, Eldon, MO 65026; 573-369-3306
starkcaverns.com

A beautiful cave in the Lake of the Ozarks region, but one tucked away from all the hustle and bustle in a lovely natural setting. Stark Caverns offers hour-long tours along well-lit paths, highlighting formations and reflective pools with a rainbow of colors that accentuate the other-worldly beauty to be found underground. Speaking of otherworldly, if you want a truly unique experience, call ahead to arrange a black light tour, one of the few available nationwide. This tour is available by reservation and focuses on the fluorescence of cave minerals. The normal lighting is extinguished and each guest carries their own black-light (and wears a helmet for safety) as your guide introduces you to the science of fluorescent minerals. A wonderful way to see caves in a whole new light.

9 Bridal Cave

526 Bridal Cave Road, Camdenton, MO 65020; 573-346-2676
bridalcave.com

You don't have to be a member of the wedding party to enjoy Bridal Cave, but after your visit you'll certainly understand why more than 3,000 couples have decided to tie the knot among the stalactites in their underground chapel. Besides weddings, this cave is known for its numerous flowing onyx formations—more than any other cave in the state, according to the website. In fact, there are so many formations of all kinds that it could take multiple tours to see them all. Bridal Cave also offers lantern tours, but only on Saturdays during the summer (advance reservations required); they do come with a souvenir caving helmet for the kids, so be sure to call ahead if you're interested. If you're inspired to plan your wedding here, all the better.

Cathedral Cave onyx formations

10 Bluff Dweller's Cave

163 Cave Road, Noel, MO 64854; 417-475-3666
bluffdwellerscave.com

One of Missouri's most remote spelunking destinations, Bluff Dweller's Cave sits only a few minutes away from both the Arkansas and Oklahoma borders. What makes this cave worth the drive is the sheer diversity in cave life and unique formations on offer making this a must-see on your Missouri Caves bucket list. Critters you may observe on your tour include five different species of salamander, three kinds of bats, frogs, albino crayfish, and more. The cave also includes plenty of formations such as stalactites, columns, and flowstone. But visitors will also see the enchanting Musical Chimes, a 10-ton balanced rock, and the longest rimstone dam in the state, creating the cave's Crystal Lake. A nice little museum provides a historical overview of the cave and hosts an impressive mineral collection.

An old railroad bridge along the Katy Trail

WITH ITS RUGGED MOUNTAINS, vast national forest, world-class rail-trails, and active urban biking scene, Missouri is a premier pedal-powered destination. No matter where you are, there are trails just waiting to show you the way as the breeze whistles through your wheels. Whether you're into mountain biking, family outings, or long-distance journeys, Missouri has you covered. Here are just a few of the amazing biking destinations in the state.

BIKING

15

4 Statewide

1 Two Rivers Bike Park

Two Rivers Road, Highlandville, MO 65669;
trailspring.org/two-rivers

A short drive south of Springfield, you'll find one of the most gorgeous and challenging mountain biking destinations around. Two Rivers is tucked in next to the James River in the rolling and rocky Ozark hills and has been professionally designed to offer an outstanding day of shredding for riders of every skill level. A dozen looping trails, rated from easy to extremely difficult, let you piece together your own dream route while also enjoying the rugged isolation of the natural Ozark landscape. There are even wooden ramps and jumps where you can practice your skills before heading off into the unknown. Admission is free, but you may also have to share the paths with runners or hikers, so keep an eye out for others.

2 Blue River Parkway Trails

Multiple access points along Blue River Road and East Blue Ridge Boulevard, Kansas City, MO
urbantrailco.com/the-trails?id=75705

One of the many extensive trail systems in Kansas City, the Blue River system comprises more than 20 miles of biking bliss. The trails run along the beautiful Blue River as it meanders through an undeveloped oasis that feels miles away from the surrounding city. Trails range from casual meanders along the creek to difficult technical trails that will test your grit and no doubt leave a little in your teeth by day's end. Multiple trails, and multiple access points to them, are scattered down Blue River Road and through the surrounding neighborhoods, so be sure to check out one of the detailed maps offered by Kansas City's Urban Trail Co., a local nonprofit trail group, to plan your day before heading out.

3 Berryman Trail

Between Potosi & Steelville, MO
gorctrails.com/trails/berryman

Want to really get away from it all? Head out to this isolated 20-plus-mile multiuse trail in the Mark Twain National Forest. The Berryman is well marked but lightly traveled, so you may have the whole thing to yourself; nevertheless, watch for hikers and horses. It's a rocky trail, with challenging climbs and exhilarating descents, and was even designated an "Epic" ride by the International Mountain Biking Association. For completionists, the ride can be broken up into two parts (utilizing Berryman and Brazil Creek Campgrounds) or done in a single day. Either way, you'll be in the wilderness, with no facilities and spotty cell reception, so bring water and snacks, along with a map in case you get turned around where the Berryman and Ozark Trails run concurrently or when crossing an occasional logging access road.

4 Katy Trail State Park

Statewide; 573-449-7402
mostateparks.com/park/katy-trail-state-park, bikekatytrail.com

An absolute gem of the Missouri park system, the Katy Trail is the longest rail-to-trail system in the entire United States. Built on a railbed running 240 miles east–west, the Katy is an easy ride over crushed gravel and each year it's used by thousands of people from all over the world. There is an extensive network of trailheads along the way, so that you can choose an easy ramble or a long-distance workout, whatever you're in the mood for. Some highlights include the Katy's only train tunnel near Rocheport (the town is lovely as well; see page 95) and the McKittrick Trailhead, which puts you near Missouri wine country and connects through a 2-mile spur to Hermann, a "picture book village" (according to its tourism website) with plenty to do and see. Suitable for all ages and skill levels.

5 Sunbridge Hills Conservation Area & Krug Park

St. Joseph, MO; Sunbridge: 816-271-3100; Krug: 816-271-5500
nature.mdc.mo.gov/discover-nature/places/sunbridge-hills-ca
mtbproject.com/trail/7002468/krug-park

Two great easy-to-intermediate mountain bike trails within only a few miles of each other in northern St. Joseph. Sunbridge overlooks the Missouri River and hosts some interesting local legends including witches' graves and cults who used to visit nearby caves. But the real draw here is a 3-mile loop trail that offers a fair challenge while also providing lovely views of the river valley. Krug Park is a short bike or car ride to the east and has a longer trail at nearly seven miles featuring several bridges, slightly more challenging terrain, and a waterfall a couple miles in if you need a place to recharge. Krug is also St. Joseph's oldest municipal park, hosting a range of activities and classic architecture that's worth a look.

7 Statewide

6 Lost Valley Trail

Weldon Spring Conservation Area, Defiance, MO 63341; 636-441-4554
gorctrails.com/trails/lost-valley

Lost Valley is a popular technical trail just outside of St. Louis, so if you feel like some company, this might be a good pick. The trail itself is a 10-plus-mile loop tucked into the Weldon Spring Conservation Area. It features single- and doubletrack, old homesteads, a cemetery, and a water crossing. The doubletrack is often graveled and easygoing, but the singletrack amps up the challenge and is what most riders come for. It's also very rocky, so bringing a repair kit is advised. The trailhead is easily accessible—it's just a few miles south of I-64 as you head west out of the city. The parking area can be easy to miss though, so be sure to keep an eye out to the north as you drive.

7 US Bicycle Route 66 & 76

Statewideadventurecycling.org/routes-and-maps/us-bicycle-route-system/maps-and-route-resources

The US Bicycle Route System (USBRS) is a national program designating connected systems of interstate routes for safer bicycle travel across the entire country. In Missouri, USBR 66 charts a bike-friendly route along historic US Route 66 as it travels through small-town USA. USBR 76 is part of the larger TransAmerica Trail, which runs from Oregon to Virginia and travels through the Ozark Mountains in Missouri. In case you're looking to try out both trails in a single day, they meet briefly in the town of Marshfield; both trails cross the entire state, so chances are wherever you live, there's one not too far away. USBR 76 is well marked, while USBR 66 is less so. Either way, it's best to bring a map and chart your course before heading out to explore Missouri's highways.

8 Frisco Highline Trail

Springfield to Willard; 417-864-2015
ozarkgreenways.org/explore/greenway-trails/frisco-highline-trail

A long and scenic rail-trail running 35 miles between Springfield and Bolivar. The Frisco Highline travels through the rolling Ozark hills, but because it sits on an old railbed, the trail remains relatively flat over its entire length. There are multiple trailheads along the way, so you can pick where and how long you want to ride. Additionally, there are many places to stop for a bite to eat or a bathroom break along the way, as well as a number of well-researched historical markers pointing out old medicinal springs, bank robberies, and even the site of a hobo campground from the Great Depression. The Frisco Highline also intersects US Bicycle Route 76 (aka the TransAmerica Trail; see previous trip) at mile 16, providing an opportunity for locals and long-haulers to mingle.

9 Swope Park Mountain Bike Trails

Swope Park, 6001 Oakwood Drive, Kansas City, MO 64132
urbantrailco.com/the-trails?id=75701

The Swope Trails are part of an ambitious plan to design and build more than 50 miles of multiuse trails within Kansas City proper. Currently, there are 12.5 miles of bike trail already in place and more on the way, eventually connecting with the Blue River Parkway Trails to the south. The existing trails are concentric loops that start with a short (0.5-mile), kid-friendly experience, then expand to a 3.5-mile beginner loop and an 8-mile intermediate loop. All trails showcase the picturesque limestone bluffs that define the topography of the park, with the 8-mile Wudchuk Run offering the most challenging technical elements in the Swope system. Nestled inside Kansas City's biggest park, these trails will trick you into forgetting the urban sprawl that surrounds this downhill paradise.

10 Wolf Creek Bike Trail

County Road 429, Poplar Bluff, MO 63901; 573-785-1475
mtbproject.com/trail/7027125/wolf-creek-trail-849

Interested in mountain biking but not ready to go rock hopping quite yet? Wolf Creek near Poplar Bluff is an excellent beginners trail that offers over 10 miles of singletrack, with good flow and a few rocks here and there to provide a nice chill day in the woods. This is a multiuse trail in the Mark Twain National Forest, so don't expect much in the way of facilities. But do expect beautiful scenery and a moderate amount of company, as the trail is just a few miles north of the city and is a well-known local retreat. Wolf Creek is a great trail for the whole family, offering a nice challenge for kids and beginners and a place to really cut loose for more-experienced riders.

Table Rock Lake in Branson

IF MISSOURI BOASTED only the confluence of two of America's biggest rivers—the Missouri and the Mississippi—that would be impressive enough. But there is so much more to Missouri's waterways and so many ways to enjoy them, it can be difficult to know where to begin. With a unique karst topography covering most of the state and acting as a natural water filter, there are nearly endless miles of clean, clear rivers and streams, giant springs, and massive creek-fed lakes to enjoy. Here are just a few of the very best ways to enjoy Missouri's wonderful watersheds.

FINDING YOUR WATERWAY

1 Sam A. Baker State Park

9729 MO 143, Patterson, MO 63956; 573-856-4411
mostateparks.com/park/sam-baker-state-park

A beautiful and quiet park tucked away deep in the Ozarks, Sam A. Baker offers a number of ways to while away a day in the woods. But the real draw here is the clean, clear water that flows down Big Creek and the St. Francis River. Take a short hike down the gorgeous shut-in tail to reach the isolated shut-in pool for a perfect swim, or bring your inner tubes if you want to float back to the park entrance. (A uniquely Ozarkian natural phenomenon, a shut-in is the result of carved rock formations diverting a river's flow into isolated streams, waterfalls, and pools.) If you're looking to spend a little more time on the water, stop at the park store to arrange a canoe or kayak float on the nearby St. Francis River. Floats run daily from April to October, but be sure to call ahead for times and river conditions.

2 Current River

Ozark National Scenic Riverways; Visitor Center: 404 Watercress Road, Van Buren, MO 63965; 573-323-4236
nps.gov/ozar

An essential floating destination, the Current River is located in the Ozark National Scenic Riverways and runs 184 miles from Montauk State Park down through Van Buren and eventually into Arkansas. Bring your own gear and put in where you like, or make a reservation with one of the numerous local outfitters that run several floats daily during warm weather. One of the best floats on the Current starts at Cedar Grove and ends at Akers; pull out just above Welch Spring to get a good look at the spring as well as the moody ruins of the old Welch Hospital. Another great run starts at Akers and ends at Pulltite, where you'll pass Cave Spring, which is so large that you can actually paddle into the cave for a cool break.

3 Table Rock Lake

Table Rock Lake State Park, 5272 MO 165, Branson, MO 65616; 417-334-4704
mostateparks.com/park/table-rock-state-park, visittablerocklake.com

Of all Missouri's lakes, Table Rock ranks among the clearest, cleanest, biggest, and most beloved and the opportunities for recreation are endless. Canoe and kayak the day away or bring your big boat if you want to do some fishing or waterskiing. Want to rent a boat or a wave runner? The full-service state park marina can help you out. There's also an old-time paddleboat, the *Branson Belle,* that offers dinner and a show as you cruise (visit silverdollarcity.com/showboat-branson for details). If you're looking for a more low-key day, bike the 2-plus-mile Lakeshore Trail, connecting the park marina and the Dewey Short Visitor Center. There are ample access paths along the way for swimming, and the visitor center is an excellently curated history of the area and the creation of the lake.

Sunset on Table Rock Lake

4 Johnson's Shut-Ins State Park

148 Taum Sauk Trail, Middle Brook, MO 63656; 573-546-2450
mostateparks.com/park/johnsons-shut-ins-state-park

Few places in Missouri draw a crowd like Johnson's Shut-Ins, and for good reason. As with other shut-ins across the state, clear water cuts through, and is trapped by, hard dolomite deposits. Johnson's Shut-Ins is unique, however, in that rather than finding a way around the rock over millions of years, the water has cut right through the middle. The result is a dramatic collection of spillways, plunge pools, and deep swimming holes. Known as "nature's water park," Johnson's Shut-Ins attracts young and old alike with its cool water and dramatic rock formations. A word of advice: In summer, avoid weekends unless you can arrive before 9 a.m. Limited parking and massive weekend crowds mean you may be waiting in line at the entrance for hours until a spot opens up for you.

5 Mina Sauk Falls

Taum Sauk Mountain State Park, State Highway CC, MO 63650; 573-546-2450
mostateparks.com/park/taum-sauk-mountain-state-park, alltrails.com/trail/us/missouri/mina-saulk-falls-trail

The route to this watery wonder is a 3-mile loop trail (about 1.5 miles to the falls, then about 1.5 to return) through mildly challenging, rocky terrain. But those who make the trek come back in awe after taking a break to soak in the highest waterfall in Missouri. A part of Taum Sauk Mountain State Park and a stop on the famous Ozark Trail, Mina Sauk Falls is a wet-weather falls and is best viewed soon after a rainstorm. When flowing, it offers a dramatic 132 feet of crashing water as it winds down through the exposed rock. But the waterfall isn't the only sight to see. The trail passes through quiet forests and open glades that offer an expansive view of the surrounding St. Francois Mountains.

6

Meramec River

Multiple counties in southeast and south-central Missouri

The Meramec is one of the longest wild rivers in Missouri and is a favorite recreation destination all along its 218 meandering miles. Some of the best places to enjoy the river are around Cuba and Steelville, the latter known as "The Floating Capital of Missouri." In this region you'll find dozens of outfitters, parks, and resources to plan your best day floating, fishing, and swimming. The Huzzah and Courtois (inexplicably pronounced "code-a-way") are nearby creeks, smaller than the Meramec, yet equally popular; all three offer pristine Ozark beauty and clear, cold water from caves and springs that dot the landscape. If you're looking to avoid the big outfitters, **Browns Canoe Rental** in Steelville (browncountycanoe.com) is a local favorite and considered a hidden gem.

Advisory: As many Missouri rivers have sections of fast flowing current and are subject to dangerous conditions during periods of high water, please exercise caution, check local water levels before a trip, and be sure to use lifejackets and common sense when enjoying Missouri's wild rivers.

A peaceful float down the Meramec River

7 Lake of the Ozarks

Several counties across central Missouri; nearby towns include Lake Ozark and Osage Beach
funlake.com

At one time the largest man-made lake in the world, Lake of the Ozarks was created by a hydroelectric dam that impounded all the waterways flowing through the region. Once complete, it immediately became a popular tourist destination for locals and out-of-staters alike. Now you can fish, swim, boat, ski, and chill out to your heart's content on the gently bobbing waves of this spring-fed treasure. There are many towns and tourist-oriented outfitters all around the lake, so it's always easy to find what you're looking for. Seeking something a bit more wild? "Party Cove"—aka Anderson Hollow Cove in Lake of the Ozarks State Park—is an unofficial hot spot described by *The New York Times* as the "oldest established permanent floating bacchanal in the country."

Early morning fishing along the Eleven Point River

8 Jacks Fork River

Ozark National Scenic Riverways; Visitor Center: 404 Watercress Road,
Van Buren, MO 63965; 573-323-4236
nps.gov/ozar

One of the two rivers that make up the Ozark National Scenic Riverways, the Jacks Fork is widely known for its wild and isolated natural
beauty. The upper 25 miles are only navigable in the spring when water
levels are high, but from Buck Hollow up to the mouth at Two Rivers,
the Jacks Fork is navigable from spring through fall. Bring your own gear
or contact one of the numerous outfitters that service the area to put
together your trip. Some highlights include Jam Up Cave, Alley Spring
and Mill, and the numerous steep bluffs that tower over the river as you
glide by. Around Two Rivers, keep an eye out and you may be lucky
enough to spot one of a few herds of wild horses that roam these hills.

9 Eleven Point River

South-central Missouri, just northeast of Alton
rivers.gov/rivers/eleven-point.php

You can't say you've explored the best of Missouri's rivers unless
you've spent a day on the Eleven Point, 138 miles of pristine river
flowing through lonely Ozark hills before crossing into Arkansas. A
recommended section of river is the 44.4-mile Eleven Point National
Scenic River between Thomasville and State Highway 142, the only
section of river in Missouri designated as Wild and Scenic by the
federal government. There are several official access points and a
small handful of outfitters in the area if you need to set up a float
or get directions. This is deep wilderness, so plan ahead and don't
count on phone reception. If you can, stop by the short Greer Spring
Trail to visit one of the largest and most pristine springs in the state.

10 Mark Twain Riverboat

100 Center St., Hannibal, MO 63401; 573-221-3222
marktwainriverboat.com

The Mighty Mississippi, arguably America's most well-known river
and the setting of many of Mark Twain's classic stories, makes up the
entirety of Missouri's eastern border. It's definitely worth a visit, and
one of the best ways to do it is aboard the *Mark Twain* Riverboat right
in the middle of Hannibal. You can choose from daily sightseeing
cruises that last an hour or dinner cruises with live music and dancing.
There's even a special Sunday lunch cruise where guests eat with the
captain; call ahead or check the website for times and reservations.
No matter which experience you choose, the real attraction is always
the rolling and roiling muddy waters of this mythic river as it carves
through the history and future of the region.

Clifty Creek north of Dixon in the Ozarks

MISSOURI HAS MORE THAN 900 trails ranging from easy urban loops to tough rocky climbs, deep wooded ravines to high mountain scrambles, and everything in between. No matter your skill level, there's always a great outing close at hand. It's never a bad season to get outside in a state so full of natural wonders, so grab your boots and take a hike.

HIKING

1 Irish Wilderness

Highway J (Camp Five Pond Trailhead), Doniphan, MO; Mark Twain National Forest, 573-364-4621
fs.usda.gov/recarea/mtnf/recarea/?recid=21728, ouachitamaps.com/Irish%20Wilderness.html, alltrails.com/trail/us/missouri/whites-creek-trail-loop-from-camp-five-pond-trailhead

A few steps into the 16,000-plus-acre Irish Wilderness is enough to make you want to turn your day trip into a long weekend. Rocky hills, caves, and creeks cover a 19th-century Irish settlement destroyed during the Civil War. Nature reclaimed the land creating Missouri's largest federally protected wilderness. The emphasis is on *wilderness* here, so come prepared. There are no facilities on-site, so bring snacks and water with you. The primary trail is White's Creek, an 18.6-mile loop, which could be done in a day if you get an early start, but if you're not feeling so ambitious, consider following the southern leg out to the Eleven Point River then back. Trail signage can be sparse, so bring along a map and a GPS if you head off the beaten path.

2 Natural Tunnel Trail at Bennett Spring

26250 MO 64A, Lebanon, MO 65536; 417-532-4338
mostateparks.com/park/bennett-spring-state-park

Well known as one of Missouri's premier trout-fishing destinations, Bennett Spring State Park offers many ways to enjoy the outdoors, including this lovely hike to a stunning geologic wonder. The Natural Tunnel Trail is a popular trail and easy to locate within the park. It travels approximately 3.35 miles through the forest and even past a neat little cave before ending at the tunnel itself. The Natural Tunnel is tall and wide, carved from the surrounding rock over thousands of years and runs about 300 feet. Be sure to explore it from end to end before turning around for the hike back. There are numerous water crossings along the way (and in the tunnel) which are often dry, but if you tackle this hike when it's wet, be sure to wear good waterproof boots.

3 Ozark Trail

Statewide from St. Louis to the Arkansas border
ozarktrail.com

The Ozark Mountains cover a vast area including parts of Oklahoma and Arkansas, a smidge of Kansas, and nearly all of southern Missouri. Since it holds the largest share of the Ozarks' acreage, it's only fitting that Missouri also has the longest hiking trail exploring this unique landscape. Currently, the OT, as it's affectionately known, has over 400 miles of completed trail, with the goal of creating a contiguous route rambling southeast between St. Louis and Arkansas. With so many miles, it's easy to find a section near you to explore for the day. The Ozark Trail Association has excellent maps and trip planners to help you plan an outing; another great resource is the guidebook *Five-Star Trails: The Ozarks* (Menasha Ridge Press). Some trail highlights include the Taum Sauk and Karkaghne sections, the latter named for a mythical dragon-like beast said to roam the hills.

4 Bell Mountain Loop Trail

Bell Mountain Wilderness, near Belleview (trailheads on Forest Service Road 2228 and State Highway A); Mark Twain National Forest, 573-364-4621
fs.usda.gov/internet/fse_documents/stelprdb5123000.pdf; alltrails.com/trail/us/missouri/bell-mountain-loop-trail

The Bell Mountain Wilderness sits in the gorgeous St. Francois Mountains near the town of Belleview. At 11.6 miles in total, Bell Mountain is a full-day walk, but it's worth it for the sheer number of unique features you'll encounter along the way. Deep forests are interspersed with pine glades featuring plenty of exposed rock and colorful lichen. There are also perennial streams that cut through rock gorges, all leading to an epic view across miles of unspoiled forest. Among the coolest things you'll see on the trail are the wild goats that often hang out near the top of the mountain. They're friendly, but they can also be aggressive, especially if you have something they want, so be sure to keep your trail mix secure when you're going for that goat selfie.

5 Devil's Icebox Trail

Rock Bridge Memorial State Park, 5901 S. MO 163, Columbia, MO 65203; 573-449-7402
mostateparks.com/park/rock-bridge-memorial-state-park

A really fun, short trail that's great for even the youngest hiker, especially if it's summertime. The Devil's Icebox is an easy loop, often following a boardwalk and including several sets of stairs leading up to the Icebox itself before heading back. Near the beginning, don't miss the left-forking spur to a natural tunnel before returning to follow the trail up past the overlooks. You'll know when you've reached the

caves by the steep, winding staircase descending into the rocks. The actual Devil's Icebox is closed to protect the bat population, but just opposite is Connor's Cave, which it's open for exploration year-round. Wear good boots if you want to keep your feet dry in the creek, and bring a flashlight—it gets dark in a hurry in there.

6 Clifty Creek Natural Area Trail

Clifty Creek Natural Area; County Road 511, Dixon, MO 65459; 573-815-7900
nature.mdc.mo.gov/discover-nature/places/clifty-creek

Described in a 19th-century geological survey as "wildly picturesque and romantic in its loneliness," Clifty Creek was Missouri's first ever official natural area, and today it's still one of the state's great hidden gems. From the parking lot trailhead on a gravel road, you'll embark on a 2.5-mile loop showcasing limestone bluffs, crystal-clear creeks, and ultimately, a massive natural bridge cut through a dolomite cliff by a now-dried-out tributary to Clifty Creek. The area is rich in wildlife, diverse species of flower and fern, and dramatic rock formations, making it a favorite of photographers. Bring your own water and food, as there are no services available. A perfect walk for those looking to slip away from the world for a while.

7 Drover's Trail

Prairie State Park; 128 NW 150th Lane, Mindenmines, MO 64769; 417-843-6711
mostateparks.com/park/prairie-state-park

Tallgrass prairie once covered most of western and northern Missouri, but now this ecosystem is nearly absent from the state. Prairie State Park is the largest remnant of Missouri's ancient prairie, and its 2.6-mile Drover's Trail is a great way to experience it. It's a mostly level loop along a mowed path, so it's nearly impossible to get lost. Late spring and summer are the best times to visit, with a riot of gorgeous wildflowers in full bloom. But in any season, definitely check out the bison before you leave. Park staff at the visitor center can usually tell you approximately where they are before you head out. Don't get too close, however: These are wild, free-roaming bison and can be dangerously aggressive, especially mothers with young calves.

8 Coy Bald Trail

Hercules Glades Wilderness, US 160 to Forest Service Road 155, Bradleyville, MO 65614; Mark Twain National Forest, 573-364-4621
fs.usda.gov/recarea/mtnf/recarea/?recid=21754

Hercules Glades is a large and impressively diverse wilderness area hidden in the hills of south-central Missouri. There are numerous trails in the wilderness, but Coy Bald is the best trail for a single day. The 6.7-mile loop travels through deep woods and open glades with amazing views of the surrounding hills before you arrive at the waterfalls and deep bedrock channel of Long Creek. Coy Bald is remote, lightly trafficked, and, at times, poorly marked. This includes the trailhead, which is obvious but can lack signage. So make sure you come prepared with a map and take care not to lose the trail, especially when crossing Long Creek. But in exchange for all that preparation, you may very well have this wilderness all to yourself.

9 Fort Belle Fontaine Loop Trail

Fort Belle Fontaine Park, 13002 Bellefontaine Road, St. Louis, MO 63138; 314-615-8800
stlouiscountymo.gov/st-louis-county-departments/parks/places/fort-belle-fontaine

If you live near St. Louis, Fort Belle Fontaine offers a fascinating and historic hike without spending hours of your day in the car. This loop trail covers a little less than 3 miles, but there's so much to see along the way, give yourself a little extra time to see it all. The former site of an early-19th-century fort, the park now houses an incredible number of stonework ruins built by the Works Progress Administration in the 1930s. In addition to crawling around the ruins, hikers can also enjoy a walk along Coldwater Creek and even the banks of the Missouri River as it prepares to meet the Mississippi just a few miles downstream. If you're feeling brave, linger near the stone stairs, where reports of ghost sightings are common.

Free roaming bison herd along Drover's Trail

George Washington Carver

LEWIS AND CLARK set a course up the Missouri River. Pioneers, traveling westward on the Oregon and Santa Fe Trails, passed through the "Gateway to the West" (aka St. Louis) in droves. When the Civil War broke out, Missouri was on the front lines. The home of Mark Twain, George Washington Carver, and more than a dozen Native American tribes, Missouri is a state with an exceptional history, just waiting to be explored.

HISTORY & CULTURE

35

1 Ste. Geneviève National Historic Park

Visitor Center: 99 S. Main St., Ste. Geneviève, MO 63670; 573-880-7189
nps.gov/stge, visitstegen.com

The oldest permanent settlement in Missouri, founded in 1735 and designated as a new national park in 2018, Ste. Geneviève is proud of its past, and it shows. You'll find some of the most well-preserved homes west of the Mississippi, including the nearly forgotten "vertical log" style. Out of only five remaining examples of this style in the US, Ste. Geneviève boasts three. All of the homes are open for tours, some led by local historians in period costume. In addition to tours, downtown also boasts unique and locally owned shops, galleries, eateries, and a new cultural museum to help you put all this history in context. A walking tour around town and along the Mississippi is the perfect way to discover how Missouri first began.

2 J. W. "Blind" Boone Home & the African American Heritage Trail

10 N. Fourth St., Columbia, MO 65201; 573-449-0039
blindboonehome.org, como.gov/parksandrec/cip/capital-improvement-project-african-american-heritage-trail

One of ragtime's greatest musicians was born and raised in Missouri. J. W. "Blind" Boone was a prodigy who could pick up and play any instrument and, it was said, could copy any tune after hearing it only once. At the Blind Boone Home, you'll be treated to an in-depth history of Boone by a member of the John William Boone Heritage Foundation and a tour of his restored 19th-century Victorian home featuring personal artifacts from Boone's life. Afterward, take a walk along the African American Heritage Trail, a 2-mile loop with plaques commemorating the history and contributions of the African American community to Columbia. Tours are by appointment only but are easy to arrange; maps for the walking tour are available on the Columbia Parks website.

3 Bollinger Mill State Historic Site

113 Bollinger Mill Road, Burfordville, MO 63739; 573-243-4591
mostateparks.com/park/bollinger-mill-state-historic-site

This enormous five-story mill on the banks of the Whitewater River is miraculously preserved, as is the original covered bridge, now used to stroll leisurely across the river for some great picture taking opportunities. Bollinger Mill was a center of commerce during the Civil War, and the site today offers a peek at the waterworks beneath, along with an agricultural and millworks museum and a small shop on the main floor. The higher floors are open for tours by on-site staff except on very hot days (usually over 94°F). The site is also recognized by the Trail of Tears Association as a significant location on that tragic route. On the grounds, there are picnic areas and a short, lovely trail leading to the nearly two-century-old Bollinger family cemetery.

4 Village of Arrow Rock

Arrow Rock, MO 65320; 660-837-3231
arrowrock.org, friendsofarrowrock.org

Unique among Missouri's historic sites, Arrow Rock is a National Historic Landmark that is also a vibrant village with a host of things to do and see. Stroll down the boardwalk to browse specialty shops and choose a place for lunch, such as the J. Huston Tavern, continuously in operation since opening in 1834. There's plenty of history as well, with four free museums and dozens of historic markers chronicling the village's role along the Santa Fe Trail, the Lewis and Clark Expedition, and the home of artist George Caleb Bingham. You can also walk the Lewis and Clark trail down to the banks of the Missouri River and catch a way-off-Broadway show at the Lyceum Theatre. Note that nearly all businesses are closed Mondays and Tuesdays, so plan your visit accordingly.

5 George Washington Carver National Monument

5646 Carver Road, Diamond, MO 64840; 417-325-4151
nps.gov/gwca

George Washington Carver was a scientist, a teacher, and a man of faith. Living through racial segregation and violence in post–Civil War America, Carver looked to nature and God in his struggle for knowledge, eventually achieving worldwide fame for his agricultural and scientific expertise. The George Washington Carver National Monument encompasses the Missouri farm where he grew up and contains extensive exhibits chronicling his inspiring life and scientific achievements, including a working replica laboratory from his professorship at Tuskegee Institute. The monument grounds include the Carver Trail, a wonderful walk through the woods, prairies, and streams that inspired young Carver to learn more about the natural world. The statues and preserved cabins along the loop further illuminate the formative years of one of the world's greatest agricultural scientists.

6 Mark Twain's Hannibal

Hannibal Convention & Visitors Bureau, 925 Grand Ave., Hannibal, MO 63401;
573-221-2477; visithannibal.com

You can't say you know about American literature without being familiar with the works of Mark Twain. He was born and raised in the town of Hannibal, where the hills, caves, and the Mighty Mississippi fueled his imagination and became important locations in some of his most famous books. Hannibal has built itself around his legacy and offers a number of immersive ways to learn more, the most prominent being the **Mark Twain Boyhood Home & Museum,** a collection of six historic properties full of exhibits and artifacts that are all accessible with one ticket (see marktwainmuseum.org for more information). Of course, you have to take a stroll down to Center Street Landing and Nipper Park to see the Mississippi roll by just as Twain did all those years ago.

7 Trail of Tears State Park

429 Moccasin Springs Road, Jackson, MO 63755; 573-290-5268
mostateparks.com/park/trail-tears-state-park

Recognized by the Cherokee Nation and the National Trail of Tears Association, this park, situated on a high bluff overlooking the Mississippi River, was created in remembrance of the journey of the Cherokee Indian tribes across Missouri during their forced removal. Head up to the overlook to see the stretch of river where native people entered Missouri on their forced march to Oklahoma in the winter of 1838–39. Be sure to stop by the Bushyhead Memorial and the visitor center to learn more about this tragic chapter in history and the individuals who left their mark on this region. If you're up for a walk, the park has trails with modest mileage that could easily be completed in an afternoon, as well as Mississippi River access for boating and fishing.

8 Gateway Arch National Park

11 N. Fourth St., St. Louis, MO 63102; 314-655-1600; nps.gov/jeff

There are few more iconic sights in America than the colossal Gateway Arch rising over 600 feet above the St. Louis skyline. The Arch is the tallest monument in the western hemisphere, but it's impossible to truly appreciate until you actually walk up and touch it yourself. Better yet, if you're brave enough and have a few extra dollars, ride the tram up to the very top. Built to commemorate St. Louis's important role in westward expansion, this history is explored in the newly renovated museum and extensive green space. Enjoy the river as it rolls by, and even take a riverboat cruise if you like. Be aware: The Arch sits in the heart of downtown, so parking can be tricky, especially on weekends or during special events.

9 Annie & Abel Van Meter State Park

32146 N. MO 122, Miami, MO 65344; 660-886-7537
mostateparks.com/park/annie-and-abel-van-meter-state-park

The first thing you'll notice are forests and hills that rise dramatically out of the surrounding cornfields, but look closer and discover that Van Meter State Park is a premier destination for learning about Native American History in the state. Immediately upon entering the park, you'll see Missouri's American Indian Cultural Center, an extensive museum and interpretive center all about the Native cultures of Missouri. There's a focus on the Otoe-Missouria tribe, whose land the park now sits upon, but the Sac, Fox, Shawnee, Osage, and other tribes are also represented. Besides the museum, there are burial mounds and ancient earthworks inside the park, easily reachable by car and scenic trails. You can also bring a picnic and go fishing or take a stroll at Lake Wooldridge before you go.

The American Indian Cutural Center at Van Meter State Park

10 Battle of Lexington State Historic Site

1101 Delaware St., Lexington, MO 64067; 660-259-4654
mostateparks.com/park/battle-lexington-state-historic-site

Missouri was a divided state during the American Civil War. With a Southern-loyalist government that favored secession, Missouri was also home to large numbers of abolitionists and Union loyalists. As a result, Missouri became the stage for many bloody conflicts. One of the most symbolic was the Battle of Lexington. Here, you can tour the Anderson House, still riddled with bullet holes and cannon fire from the three-day siege that took place there. There are guided tours for a nominal fee and a free museum that thoroughly lays out the details of the battle which saw the house change hands between Union and Confederate soldiers multiple times. The surrounding town of Lexington also contains an extensive amount of Civil War history that is worth exploring while you're in town.

11 America's National Churchill Museum

501 Westminster Ave., Fulton, MO 65251; 573-592-5369
nationalchurchillmuseum.org

In the small, rural town of Fulton sits one of the most astonishing, engaging, and unexpected museums in the entire state. The origins of America's National Churchill Museum date back to 1946, when Churchill delivered his famous "Iron Curtain Speech" at Fulton's Westminster College. Today the museum incorporates history with imaginative interactive exhibits that often incorporate modern technology in ways that are engaging and educational for all ages. Visitors follow a winding path as they feel themselves moving through Churchill's life and the battlegrounds of world wars one and two. Above the museum, an entire church, over 300 years old, was moved here stone by stone after the Blitz left London in tatters after the war. To top it off, eight sections of the infamous Berlin Wall are installed on the grounds as well.

Winston Churchill Memorial in Fulton

12 Missouri State Penitentiary

115 Lafayette St., Jefferson City, MO 65101; 866-998-6998
missouripentours.com

Formerly the primary center of incarceration for the entire state, the now-closed Missouri State Penitentiary offers an eerie and disturbing look inside what was once known as "the bloodiest 47 acres in America." With its ancient Gothic stonework, rusting bars, and original gas chamber, the site is a mix of gorgeous ruins and grisly history. Visitors can choose from several experiences and tour lengths, which include photography tours focusing on architecture, history tours that have almost 200 years of stories to tell, and ghost tours focused on paranormal activities (which can be arranged to last an entire night if you're up for it). Be sure to book ahead on the website, as tours often sell out.

A peaceful Amish farm near Jamesport

MISSOURI HAS ALWAYS been an agricultural state. From the vast, fertile plains of the north to the hardscrabble family homesteads that dot the Ozark hills, farms and rural life are well represented across the state. In an age when fewer and fewer families still have that connection to the land, Missouri is a leader in agritourism, providing a number of wonderful opportunities to get down on the farm.

DOWN ON THE FARM

1 Baker Creek Heirloom Seeds & Pioneer Village

2278 Baker Creek Road, Mansfield, MO 65704; 417-924-8917
rareseeds.com

Jere and Emilee Gettle have dedicated their lives to seeds and plants. It started with a single seed catalog but has grown to include festivals, workshops, and a home-grown Pioneer Village that is an absolute must visit if you've ever had a garden. The village was built as a gathering spot for anyone who cares about food or self-sufficiency, or is just feeling a little nostalgic for the simpler times. During festivals, visitors, vendors, and artisans flood the streets, and you can listen to live music and learn more about the art of growing things. On other days, it's a quiet stroll through the past. Explore the buildings, exhibits, and stores, especially the seed store. Then check out the heirloom chickens and pet the cows while you take in the countryside.

2 YaYa's Alpaca Farm

30200 E. 275th St., Garden City, MO 64747; 816-213-7555
yayasalpacafarm.com

You have to meet these sweet alpacas

Alpacas come from the mountains of South America, but because of their warm, luxurious fleece, Missouri farmers have been importing them for years. YaYa's Alpaca Farm, in a beautiful, rural setting just an hour south of Kansas City, keeps a herd of around a couple dozen and offers 90-minute tours throughout the week. Tours go all around the farm and include feeding and petting the alpacas. The owners are friendly and knowledgeable, making the tour a learning experience as well, more than worth the small fee per person. There is also a farm store where you can pick up some alpaca fiber goods if you like. One note: This is a working farm, so tours are strictly by appointment. Luckily, reservations can be made anytime on YaYa's website.

3 Grant's Farm

10501 Gravois Road, St. Louis, MO 63123; 314-577-2626
grantsfarm.com

Less a farm than a farm-themed amusement park, Grant's Farm is a favorite destination for families looking for an up-close animal experience. Originally the homestead of Ulysses S. Grant, the land is now owned by Anheuser-Busch and run as a free attraction for the public, featuring many different farm and exotic animals. Visitors are encouraged to interact with the animals, and there are even opportunities to feed parakeets and goats. You can meet the famous Budweiser Clydesdales, ride a carousel and a real camel, visit a cabin hand-built by Grant himself, and grab lunch in an authentic Bavarian courtyard. *Note:* Although admission to the farm is free, on-site parking is not, and there are small fees for extra attractions like the carousel and animal feeding.

4 Purina Farms

500 William Danforth Way, Gray Summit, MO 63039; 888-688-7387
purina.com/about-purina/purina-farms

One of the world's most recognizable brands, Purina, also operates this attraction that offers a whole day's worth of animal entertainment. In keeping with the farm theme, there are wagon rides, cow-milking demonstrations twice a day, and a hay-loft play area for the kids. There is also an animal barn with a baby-animal petting area where you can get to know a number of adorable critters including pigs, chickens, and rabbits. Plenty of dogs and cats call Purina Farms home as well. In the Pet Center, an interactive exhibit explores our relationship with our pets and houses a 20-foot-tall multilevel cat house. Daily dog shows feature diving, agility, and herding demonstrations, and there's so much more. Bonus: Parking and admission are free except on event days.

5 Green Dirt Farm

1099 Welt St., Weston, MO 64098; 816-386-2156
greendirtfarm.com

There are fewer than 200 sheep milk farms in the entire US, despite the fact that sheep's milk is far more nutritious than cow's milk and creates some truly amazing cheese. If you're curious about this mysteriously rare delicacy, a great place to learn (and taste) more is Green Dirt Farm. A tour of the farm starts at the shop and creamery, then heads out to the farm, where you'll meet some of the happiest sheep you've ever seen. After roaming the farm, you'll take a look inside the milking parlor and peek into the cheese kitchen where the magic happens. Afterward you'll head back to the shop for what many consider the best part: a complimentary tasting that is the perfect capper on this truly farm-to-table experience.

6 Amish Community, Jamesport

Jamesport, MO 64648; Jamesport Community Association, 660-684-6146
https://jamesport-mo.com/

Visiting an Amish community is a way to feel as if you've stepped into a place out of time and into living example of the good old days. There are several Amish communities throughout Missouri, but none offers quite the access of the one in Jamesport. The town is full of the usual Amish-run business dealing in bulk foods, bakeries, country goods, antiques, and more. But if you're really looking to immerse yourself in the Amish way of life, a few locals offer tours that will take you inside an Amish household to show you the inner workings of the farm and lives of the people there. These communities value their privacy, so this opportunity is truly unique. Contact the Jamesport Community Association for maps and to contact a tour guide.

7 Where Pigs Fly Farm & Pigs Aloft Museum

2810 US 50 E., Linn, MO 65051; 314-241-3488
wherepigsflyfarm.com

At this 67-acre animal paradise, you can get up close and personal with one of the sweetest menageries ever assembled. Operated as a rescue for animals in need, Where Pigs Fly is home to every kind of farm critter, plus a few creatures you wouldn't normally find on a farm—and all of them are ready to be your new best friend. The owners of the farm have created an immersive experience where animals aren't always behind a fence, often sharing space with you so you can pet, feed (a sleeve of crackers is provided with admission), and even get your first kiss from an alpaca. The small admission fee also covers your entry into North America's only pig museum, the Bird House, and more. Weekend hours are listed on the website, and weekday tours are also available by appointment.

8 Neosho National Fish Hatchery

520 Park St., Neosho, MO 64850; 417-451-0554
fws.gov/midwest/neosho

When people think of farms, animals like chickens and cows quickly spring to mind. But fish are also an important environmental and agricultural resource, and Missouri plays host to several large-scale hatcheries, including the oldest federal hatchery in the country at Neosho. Start at the visitor center to meet some of the fish raised here and experience the interactive exhibits. Then head out to explore the grounds and feed the fish as you pass numerous spring-fed ponds. There is also a walking trail and several picnic tables if you want to bring along a lunch. For a more in-depth experience, call ahead to arrange a tour with a staff biologist, which will allow you to visit the building where ongoing efforts are underway to save the endangered pallid sturgeon.

9 Warm Springs Ranch

25270 MO 98, Boonville, MO 65233; 888-972-5933
warmspringsranch.com

The official breeding farm of the famous Budweiser Clydesdales, Warm Springs Ranch is all about big horses and beer. With 300 acres and dozens of iconic Clydesdales roaming the landscape, this makes an excellent destination for anyone who loves seeing happy, healthy horses living their best lives. As Warm Springs is a breeding facility, you can see horses at every stage of life, see the foaling barn, and explore the pastures where the horses roam free. There is a fee for the tours, and reservations in advance are required (tours tend to fill up fast, so plan ahead). Each tour allows for interaction with the Clydesdales, whose size and charisma are hard to appreciate unless you meet them for yourself. Adults also get a free Budweiser sample with admission.

Klepzig Mill in the Ozark National Scenic Riverways

THE OZARKS ARE a mountain playground with endless opportunities for outdoor adventure and old-time fun. Many attractions found in the Ozarks pertain to waterways, hiking, caving, and other categories in this book. But there are some destinations so unique, so peculiarly specific to this place and the folklore that abides in these hollers, that they can only be classified as Ozarkian.

THE OZARKS

1 Ozark National Scenic Riverways

Southeast Missouri; Visitor Center: 404 Watercress Road, Van Buren, MO 63965; 573-323-4236
nps.gov/ozar

Only a few generations ago, the land surrounding the Current and Jacks Fork Rivers was a hardscrabble yet bustling agricultural community. This proud past has left behind several architectural remnants, all of which can be seen in a single day. Alley Mill is a wonderfully preserved multistory grist mill open for self-guided tours. Nichols Cabin is the remains of several buildings of a working farm from nearly 100 years ago. Klepzig Mill sits deep in the countryside and is a ruin surrounded by magnificent natural beauty. All three of these sites are free to visit; have short, beautiful trails; and are easily accessible from parking. Be sure to stop by the visitor center for an area map and to discover so much more.

2 Mingo National Wildlife Refuge

24279 MO 51, Puxico, MO 63960; 573-222-3589
fws.gov/refuge/mingo

The Ozarks once contained extensive wetlands hidden in the deep forests. But logging and draining them for agriculture irreversibly transformed nearly all of those acres. Today, the Mingo Refuge represents one of the state's few remaining ancient swamps. Take a stroll on the Boardwalk Trail, which takes you deep into the swamp ecosystem, and stop by the visitor center to learn more. But be sure to save time for the Ozark Auto Tour before you go. It's a 17-mile drive down a one-way gravel road that takes you through the backcountry of this extensive 21,500-acre preserve. The best stop along the way is the trail to the Sweet Family Cabin, just after you cross Stanley Creek. It's a short, easy hike to a restored homestead dating back to frontier times.

3 Laura Ingalls Wilder Historic Home & Museum

3060 State Highway A, Mansfield, MO 65704; 877-924-7126
lauraingallswilderhome.com

Located on the actual Rocky Ridge Farm where Laura wrote the Little House books, this historic site is a look at a real Ozark homestead that also happens to be the home of one of America's most beloved authors. Start at the Laura Ingalls Wilder–Rose Wilder Lane Museum, a well-curated collection with items that appeared prominently in the books, including Pa's actual fiddle. Then tour the farmhouse where Laura and her husband, Almanzo Wilder, lived, and even visit her writing room. Later, walk the paved trail to the Rock House. This path winds through idyllic farmland and woods as it immerses you in the countryside of Laura's life and books. For a special treat, plan your visit for late July or early August, and pluck an apple from the orchard near the farmhouse to enjoy on your way.

4 Ha Ha Tonka State Park

1491 State Highway D, Camdenton, MO 65020; 573-346-2986
mostateparks.com/park/ha-ha-tonka-state-park

Only the skeleton of an imposing estate remains atop the bluffs over-looking the Lake of the Ozarks. But its tragic history, along with the mysterious beauty of the ruins and the stunning natural setting, makes Ha Ha Tonka a must-visit in Missouri. Built in the early 20th century, the mansion was constructed by a wealthy family who even flew in Euro-pean stone masons to realize their vision for a true castle. Today, visitors are invited to explore the ruins of that dream and enjoy nearly 4,000 acres of natural beauty that inspired its construction. Numerous trails offer up-close and panoramic views of the ruins and delve deep into the surrounding forests. Picnic areas, playgrounds, and boat access to the Lake of the Ozarks offer many possibilities to build your visit.

5 Assumption Abbey

Ava, MO 65608; 417-683-5110
assumptionabbey.org

A place of austere religious observance, and the source of some of the world's finest fruitcakes, Assumption Abbey is not your typical day trip destination. Located in a beautiful and remote region of the Ozarks, the abbey is an active community of Trappist monks devoted to prac-ticing their faith in silent fellowship. Visitors are welcome to take part in prayer within the chapel and explore the monastery grounds while reflecting on their own lives and faith. There is also a small self-serve gift shop where you can purchase their astoundingly delicious fruit-cake as well as other items. *Note:* This is the monks' home, graciously open to visitors—not a tourist destination for clicking cameras or noisy kids. Please visit only if you seek a spiritual retreat and are prepared to observe complete silence.

The ancient sentinels of Elephant Rocks State Park

WHEN WAS THE LAST time you really played? Or laughed with carefree delight, completely living in the present moment? If you're traveling in Missouri, whether with kids or not, there are opportunities throughout the state to indulge your inner child. Don't be surprised if, at some of these stops, you find yourself whooping it up as you come to realize that age truly is just a state of mind.

KIDS OF ALL AGES

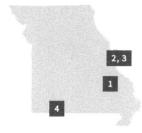

1 Elephant Rocks State Park

7406 MO 21, Belleview, MO 63623; 573-546-3454
mostateparks.com/park/elephant-rocks-state-park

Want to feel like a kid again or get your own youngsters to forget about "screen time" for a while? Then take a trip to Elephant Rocks, one of Missouri's most stunning outdoor playgrounds and an absolute must-see-to-believe in the Show-Me State. Massive granite boulders, some weighing several hundred tons, formed approximately one billion years ago and still dominate the landscape today. Wear your grippiest shoes and join in the fun of climbing, leaping, and squeezing through natural tunnels and over acres of mini mountains. Don't miss climbing to the top and getting an unspoiled view of Ozark hills for miles around or exploring tadpole pools carved into the rock. There's also a paved path around the main area for those who simply wish to marvel at this awesome geologic anomaly.

2 City Museum

750 N. 16th St., St. Louis, MO 63103; 314-231-2489
citymuseum.org

You've never been to a museum like this. Housed in the industrial husk of an old shoe factory, the City Museum is a gorgeous 10-story playground in the heart of St. Louis where exhibits take the form of massive slides, multistory sculptures that hide labyrinthine tunnels, and an entire underground cave system. Nearly everything you'll see and climb—no DO NOT TOUCH signs here—is made from industrial salvage and the artistic eye of an army of sculptors, welders, and artisans from every conceivable background. Some don't miss exhibits include the rooftop Ferris wheel and the 10-story slide. Bring an appetite for adventure, an appreciation for the surreal, and comfortable clothes for exploring the unknown. You'll definitely get lost more than once, and you'll love every surprising minute of it.

A red panda peeks out at the St. Louis Zoo

3 Saint Louis Zoo

1 Government Drive, St. Louis, MO 63110; 314-781-0900
stlzoo.org

Not only is this a huge, world-class zoo, filled with enough exhibits to dizzy the most demanding animal aficionado, it's also free, making it an easy choice when you're looking for something fun to do. Be sure to check out the new polar bear habitat and the underwater sea lion tunnel while also marveling at great apes, exploring the insectarium, and enjoying the elephants. *Note:* Although admission to the zoo is free, some supplemental attractions are not, including the zoo train, children's zoo, carousel, sea lion show, and stingray touch tank. So bring a few dollars if you want to enjoy these extras, or show up as soon as the zoo opens and experience the carousel, children's zoo, and stingrays for free as well, though it's only for the first hour.

4 Silver Dollar City

399 Silver Dollar City Parkway, Branson, MO 65616; 800-888-7277
silverdollarcity.com/theme-park

Do you like your theme parks to put as much effort into the theme as they do their heart-stopping thrill rides? Silver Dollar City has enough terrifying roller coasters and drenching water rides to keep you busy all day long, but the park is also modeled as an 1880s frontier experience that's incorporated into every aspect of the park. Enjoy old-timey live music, blacksmithing demonstrations, general-store candy shops, and the rides themselves with names like Outlaw Run and The Giant

Barn Swing. There are real log cabins and frontier churches tucked in among the wide boardwalks, plus enough varieties of funnel cake to please the pickiest sweet tooth. Admission to Marvel Cave (see Caves, page 11) is also included with each ticket, making this park well worth the price.

5 Maramec Spring Park

21880 Maramec Spring Drive, St. James, MO 65559; 573-265-7387
maramecspringpark.com

One of Missouri's most enchanting and laid-back parks, Maramec Spring offers many outdoor activities everyone will enjoy. The main attraction is the spring itself, which pumps around 100 million gallons of fresh water per day and serves as an on-site trout hatchery. Take a leisurely walk around the beautiful spring, and bring some quarters so you can feed the trout that are born and raised in the nearby spring-fed hatchery pools. If you're so inclined, bring your pole (and your fishing license) and see if you can catch one in the downstream fishing area. The park also offers free museums on agriculture and the history of the park, playgrounds and picnic tables aplenty, and trails including one through the old ironworks, whose impressive stone chimneys still stand 100 years later.

6 Six Flags St. Louis

4900 Six Flags Road, Eureka, MO 63025; 636-938-5300
sixflags.com/stlouis

Known for its continuous innovation in the field of scaring you senseless, Six Flags has a nationally renowned theme park right outside St. Louis. There are nods to Looney Tunes characters, like Bugs Bunny and Tweety, especially in the shops and kids' area, but most visitors come here to experience the wide variety of rides that will get you screaming with equal parts fear and delight. This includes many modern superhero-themed attractions such as Batman: The Ride but also features a traditional wooden coaster that's been in operation since 1976. Six Flags is an unparalleled day of excitement, but it can get expensive if you're bringing the family—it's a good idea to plan ahead and check the website, which often has good deals on tickets.

7

Wonders of Wildlife National Museum & Aquarium

500 W. Sunshine St., Springfield, MO 65807; 888-222-6060
wondersofwildlife.org

Although it only opened in 2017, Wonders of Wildlife has already been voted America's Best Aquarium by *USA Today*, and rightfully so. Adjacent to Springfield's famous Bass Pro Shop (and founded by Bass Pro Shops CEO Johnny Morris), this sprawling complex promises a trip around the world. It delivers on that promise with a huge multilevel aquarium that covers every imaginable aquatic habitat, from the open ocean to rivers to swamps and more. In addition to the aquarium, dozens of wildlife and special exhibits offer impressively detailed journeys into ecosystems including the African savanna, polar tundra, and American forests, just to name a few. Interactive and educational opportunities abound as you marvel at the natural world and make your way from sea to mountaintop—all in the space of an afternoon.

The new polar bear exhibit at the St. Louis Zoo

Kids of
All Ages

One of the endless waterfalls at Johnson Shut Ins

THE KARST FEATURES that define most of Missouri's topography makes the state a geological wonderland and a rockhound's paradise. Creeks and cliffs all across the state expose a wide variety of rock types created by ancient inland oceans, volcanic activity, and millennia of natural erosion. Caves are one popular way to explore Missouri's geology (see Caves, page 6), but there are also exciting destinations to be found in the light of day.

ROCKS & MINERALS

1 Hawn State Park

12096 Park Drive, Ste. Geneviève, MO 63670; 573-883-3603
mostateparks.com/park/hawn-state-park

Travel just an hour south of St. Louis, and you'll feel like you're a hundred miles from nowhere. One of Missouri's most tranquil getaways, Hawn State Park is nearly 5,000 acres of solitude, trails, and backwoods adventure. Of particular interest in this park is its highly diverse geology, which includes large outcroppings of streamside igneous, sedimentary, and metamorphic rock (a rarity for Missouri) along the mossy Pickle Creek Trail. In contrast, there is also a large deposit of unique LaMotte sandstone in the LaMotte Sandstone Barrens within the park. Erosion of the sandstone left behind picturesque cliffs, knobs, and valleys that create sunny, open glades filled with ancient lichen. Unlike Pickle Creek, the Barrens have no trails leading directly to them, so inquire at the park office for directions.

2 Missouri Mines State Historic Site

4000 MO 32, Park Hills, MO 63601; 573-431-6226
mostateparks.com/park/missouri-mines-state-historic-site

When you hear "historic site," do you picture single-room log cabins or a lonely informative plaque? At the Missouri Mines State Historic Site, you'll enjoy views of a sprawling industrial ruin complete with broken windows and covered in a wonderful patina of rust. An unfortunately small portion of the grounds is open to visitors, but you can still get an up-close look and some very interesting buildings that make up this former mining complex. Check out the impressive on-site museum, which includes real mining machinery and an exhaustive mineral and fossil exhibit. There's even a souvenir shop if you want to take a piece of Missouri's underground home. Don't forget to ask about the promotional film that the St. Joseph Lead Company made back in the 1950s—it's not to be missed.

Joplin Museum Complex

504 S. Schifferdecker Ave., Joplin, MO 64801; 417-623-1180
joplin-museum.org

Also known as the Joplin History & Mineral Museum, this unassuming
brick building houses an impressive collection of geologic wonders.
Half of the complex is devoted to the Tri-State Mineral Museum, which
exhibits huge displays of locally extracted minerals, including many
colorful crystals. There are also historical as well as modern exhibits on
the history and legacy of mining in the area, a look at fluorescent minerals that glow under the right lighting conditions, and a fossil exhibit.
When you're finished with minerals, don't forget that your ticket also
includes admission to the other half of the complex. This is an eclectic
and sometimes peculiar mix of smaller museums, including (but not
limited to) exhibits about cookie cutters and Bonnie and Clyde, a large
doll collection, and a circus room with an animatronic miniature circus.

A mining exhibit at the Joplin Museum

Rocks &
Minerals

4 Grand Gulf State Park

State Highway W, Koshkonong, MO 65692; 417-264-7600
mostateparks.com/park/grand-gulf-state-park

Just north of the Arkansas border, a remote farming community hides a unique geological curiosity. Known as Missouri's "Little Grand Canyon," Grand Gulf was formed by a collapsed cave and is a nearly mile-long chasm with walls as high as 130 feet. Visitors can learn about the geology on well-researched interpretive plaques before heading down the trail, which offers views from above the gulf. But the real fun is walking along the bottom and experiencing the mossy wonder of the gulf, including passing through the natural bridge tunnel that spans over 200 feet at about the halfway point of your hike. There is no official trail down into the gulf, and it can be slippery, but the park allows such exploration, advising visitors to exercise "extreme caution" when heading down. (Note: The park office is in nearby Thayer; the park, however, is in Koshkonong.)

5 Elephant Rocks State Park

7406 MO 21, Belleview, MO 63623; 573-546-3454
mostateparks.com/park/elephant-rocks-state-park

Also listed as a fun family getaway in the Kids of All Ages section (page 54), Elephant Rocks is more than an outdoor playground—it's also window into geologic time. The granite boulders that define the park were formed deep underground by cooling magma over a billion years ago, then slowly exposed by natural erosion. Wind, rain, and even the lichens that cover the rocks continue to shape the rock as they have for millennia. The site is considered a tor, a geologic term for a sudden eruption of rounded boulders from the surrounding countryside. Elephant Rocks is one of less than a dozen in the US and one of even fewer that offer an easily accessible trail, so you can get close enough to touch and examine these granite titans to your heart's content.

Rocks & Minerals

6 Devil's Honeycomb on Hughes Mountain

13706 State Highway M, Irondale, MO 63648; 636-441-4554
nature.mdc.mo.gov/discover-nature/places/hughes-mountain

Hughes Mountain Natural Area encompasses over 400 acres in the picturesque St. Francois Mountains and contains a single marked trail which leads 1.6 miles to the top of the mountain. The trail is lovely on its own, traveling through wildflower glades and up the rocky slopes, but is of special interest to the geologically minded because of the many rare polygonal columns of rhyolite found at the end of the trail. These columns formed more than a billion years ago when the volcanic rock began to cool, causing vertical movement and geometric fractures that resemble a honeycomb when viewed from above. The famous basalt columns of Ireland's Giant's Causeway were formed by the same geologic forces; however, this one is only a short drive away and far from the tourist crush.

A wooded glen at Elephant Rocks

Rocks & Minerals

7 **Sheffler Rock Shop & Geode Mine**

26880 Topanga Canyon Blvd., Kahoka, MO 63445; 319-795-5013
shefflerrockshop.com

Northeastern Missouri is often overlooked by travelers, but for
rockhounds who want to add pounds of top-shelf geodes to their
collections, Sheffler Rock Shop and Geode Mine is a must-visit destination. The mine is located inside the geologic borders of the Warsaw
Formation, known for its high-quality Keokuk geodes and offers a
true hands-on approach to visitors. For $25, you'll be led toward
the back of a cornfield and turned loose into what is basically a
shallow open-pit mine to find your fortune. The only requirement
is that you bring your own tools (rock hammer, bucket, pry bar,
etc.), as none are provided or available. The fee allows for the
harvest of 25 pounds of geodes and beyond that, visitors are left
to a blissful afternoon, digging to their heart's content.

8 **Tiemann Shut-Ins at Millstream Gardens State Forest**

Private Road 9534, Polk Township, MO 63645; 573-290-5730
nature.mdc.mo.gov/discover-nature/places/millstream-gardens-ca

The rock-minded visitor can spend weeks, months, even years exploring the amazing geological variety Missouri has to offer. But if you
have only a single day, no location offers a more robust variety of
exposed igneous rock than Tiemann Shut-Ins. The Shut-Ins are accessible down an easy paved trail, but you'll need to scramble the rest
of the way down to the St. Francis River where it cuts through the
shut-ins. Once you're among the rocks, you'll find ample examples of
exposed plutons (crystalized igneous rock) along with basalt, rhyolites,
and more which mingle along the stream bed like a geology textbook
brought to life.. This is a lightly used trail, so chances are you'll have
plenty of solitude to study the relationships between these volcanic
wonders among the quiet beauty of the waterfalls and forests.

Rocks & Minerals

A closeup of the "honeycomb" on top of Hughes Mountain

The National Museum of Transportation in St. Louis

MISSOURI HAS ALWAYS been a state on the move. Whether it was the Lewis and Clark expedition, wagon trains on the Santa Fe and Oregon Trails, the Transcontinental Railroad, Mississippi steamboat traffic, or cruising Route 66, the roads, rails, and rivers here have always been transportation hot spots. This spirit is still on display in several destinations guaranteed to inspire you to add your own travels to this rich history.

PLANES, TRAINS & AUTOMOBILES

Various locations

1 Branson Scenic Railway

206 E. Main St., Branson, MO 65616; 800-287-2462
bransontrain.com

Missouri road trips often lead to Branson, one of Missouri's top get-aways, but the Branson Scenic Railway will have you itching to leave on the next train. The journey starts at the old Branson Depot, built in 1905 and still selling tickets a hundred years later. The train is also a historical gem, with fully restored cars dating from the 1930s through the 1960s, including a concession car and bubble-top passenger cars that offer a wide-angle view of the trestles, tunnels, and wild Ozark countryside. Another unique feature here is that there are two available routes. Your train may head north through the James River Valley or south into Arkansas and over the famed Barren Fork Trestle. You may want to ride twice just so you can see it all.

2 The National Museum of Transportation

2933 Barrett Station Road, St. Louis, MO 63122; 314-965-6212
tnmot.org

It's only fitting that St. Louis, known as the "Gateway to the West," would be home to The National Museum of Transportation. This 42-acre site is home to trains, cars, boats, and planes aplenty, with a focus on hands-on experiences as guests explore the history and evolution of transportation in America. There is a major focus on trains here, with over 70 locomotives and many more individual train cars, some dating back decades before the Civil War. There's even an 1800s train tunnel on-site. Besides trains, there is a wealth of automotive history, authentic military planes, and a river tugboat. There are multiple educational STEAM (science, technology, engineering, art, and mathematics) exhibits that are fun no matter your age, plus a vast transportation library and archive if you're looking for an even deeper dive into the subject.

3 St. Louis Iron Mountain & Southern Railway

252 E. Jackson Blvd., Jackson, MO 63755; 573-243-1688
slimrr.com

A lovely train ride near Cape Girardeau with a lot of personality, the St. Louis Iron Mountain & Southern Railway offers something new each time. The train and passenger cars are nearly 100 years old, assuring an authentic old-time train experience. The ride itself is only 5 miles down and back on a decommissioned track, but every ride has a unique theme to experience. Weekly rides, offered only on Saturdays, might include chocolate tastings, dinosaurs, or James Gang train robberies with actors in period costume; all include a stop at the Cactus Gulch old-time village. Occasional evening offerings include the highly popular Murder Mystery Dinner Train, which often sells out months in advance. Check the website to reserve seats for an outing that's perfect for your crew.

4 Missouri River Runner

Amtrak, between St. Louis and Kansas City; multiple stations and stops; 800-872-7245
amtrak.com/missouri-river-runner-train

Missouri train travel isn't merely a relic of the past: There's also a great modern train experience waiting inside the Show-Me State. The *Missouri River Runner* is the intrastate Amtrak route running east–west between St. Louis and Kansas City with several stops, so you can find one close where you can hop on and another to explore. If you like, you can fit a whole round-trip between the two big cities into one long day, with a layover of a few hours in your destination city. Or you can stop off at a station of your choice and linger a while longer before catching the return train home. Some popular stops include the old-world charm and wineries of Hermann (see page 95) and Jefferson City with the bustling state capitol overlooking the Missouri River.

5 Belton, Grandview & Kansas City Railroad

502 E. Walnut St., Belton, MO 64012; 816-331-0630
kcrrm.org

A great old heritage railroad, the Belton, Grandview & Kansas City offers a short excursion and an authentic experience without any gimmicks. Originally part of the St. Louis–San Francisco Railway, this trip travels through the small town of Benton, generally about 15–20 minutes out from and back to the station. It's the shortest of the short-line excursions in the state; this one, however, comes the closest to re-creating the experience of riding the rails 100 years ago. There

are no themes or costumes, no climate control or other modern comforts. It's just you and the old diesel engine, windows down and chugging through history. To round out the trip, check out the historic Benton courthouse and grab lunch at a locally owned restaurant.

6 Nicholas-Beazley Aviation Museum

1985 S. Odell Ave., Marshall, MO 65340; 660-886-2630
nicholasbeazley.org

The Nicholas-Beazley Airplane Company was a locally owned business that designed and built prop aircraft in the 1920s and '30s. The catastrophic economic forces of the Great Depression drove them out of business, but thanks to the ongoing efforts at the Nicholas-Beazley Aviation Museum, they are far from a forgotten piece of history. The museum features meticulously restored Nicholas-Beazley planes, along with well-curated exhibits that work to preserve local aviation history, with extensive displays focused on everything from the original sales catalogues to the propeller shop to a recreation of the old manufacturing plant. There are also numerous interactive exhibits, with a focus on "young aviators," that are excellent educational introductions to the world of flight. You may even see a plane take off at the municipal airport right next door.

7 Auto World Museum

200 Peacock Drive, Fulton, MO 65251; 573-642-2080
autoworldmuseum.com

It can be easy to overlook the plain, stark white warehouse that contains the Auto World Museum, located off US 54 as it turns to bypass Fulton. But to do so would mean missing out on a gearhead's dream collection of rare and antique automobiles hidden in plain sight. The collection consists of a rotating exhibition of over 80 cars from modern times and dating back to the turn of the 20th century, with each era marked by Hollywood-style backdrops that add to the charm. The museum is light on frills, but that's OK—the cars are the real star here. Even if you're not that into automotive history, the admission fee is worth it to get your picture taken sitting in a real DeLorean (flux capacitor not included).

The Auto World Museum in Fulton

8 The Space Museum & The Grissom Center

116 E. School St., Bonne Terre, MO 63628; 573-358-1200
space-mo.org

If your interest in human ingenuity aims above and beyond the surly bonds of Earth, The Space Museum and The Grissom Center are an ideal destination for terrestrial explorers. Named for Virgil "Gus" Grissom, NASA astronaut and the second American to fly into outer space, this museum offers extensive exhibits on the history of space travel, including space suits, moon rocks, and much more. What makes the museum especially enjoyable is the enthusiasm and generosity of its founder, Earl Mullins, who has filled the facility with genuine astronaut artifacts, along with space-race cultural ephemera that defined a generation of Americans. Earl often accompanies tours with tales of how he amassed such a massive collection, and he allows visitors to touch and even try on certain artifacts, including an astronaut's glove worn on an actual space flight.

Take a seat at Busch Stadium

MISSOURIANS TAKE THEIR passion for competition in every possible direction. From the shadow of the Gateway Arch to the quiet valleys of the Ozarks, there are endless ways to enjoy a spirited contest of wills in the Show-Me State. Whether putting for par on a mountaintop, taking a historical trek through one of many sports-focused museums, or enjoying a one-on-one struggle between man and fish, there's something for everyone here.

SPORTS

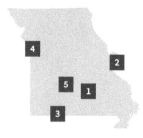

1 Montauk State Park

345 County Road 6670, Salem, MO 65560; 573-548-2201
mostateparks.com/park/montauk-state-park

Montauk State Park sits at the headwaters of the Current River and boasts both historical and natural significance, making it an outstanding outdoor destination. But what really sets this park apart is the trout hatchery that stocks the river and brings in anglers from all over to enjoy a chance at catching a whopper, or at least dinner. The hatchery is open for self-guided tours during daylight hours and is a fun way to get up close and personal with these beautiful fish. Once you're ready to bait your hook, there are several parking areas around the park reserved for fisherfolk. You can fish from the bank or wade into the cold, blue water to try your luck. Fishing licenses and trout tags are available at the on-site concessionaire.

2 St. Louis Cardinals Hall of Fame & Museum

700 Clark Ave., St. Louis, MO 63102; 314-345-9600
mlb.com/cardinals/cardinals-nation/hall-of-fame-and-museum

If you've ever talked baseball with a Cardinals fan, you've probably experienced firsthand the passion that fuels what is known as Redbird Nation. In Ballpark Village, a massive food, drink, and baseball-themed district next to Busch Stadium, you can discover the history of this fandom at the St. Louis Cardinals Hall of Fame and Museum. Exhibits include an in-depth look at the Cardinals' 11 World Series titles plus jerseys and relics from Cardinal superstars like Stan Musial and Ozzie Smith. There are also interactive opportunities like the Broadcast Booth, where aspiring announcers can record their own play-by-play of famous Cardinals moments, and Holding History, where visitors can hold game-used bats from famous players and real championship rings. Admission is free, so come experience everything this amazing museum has to offer.

3 Top of the Rock Golf Course

150 Top of the Rock Road, Ridgedale, MO 65739; 800-225-6343
bigcedar.com/golf/top-of-the-rock-course

Missouri has its share of great places to hit the links, but one truly stands out as a world-class golfing destination right in the middle of the heartland. Located at Big Cedar Lodge on Table Rock Lake, Top of the Rock is a Jack Nicklaus Signature Course that's on many golfers' bucket lists. The layout includes nine holes, each a par 3, which incorporate the surrounding Ozark topography in beautiful ways. You'll see creeks, waterfalls, and stunning views of the lake on each hole, along with surprises such as Arnold Palmer's 150-year-old barn, moved all the way here from Pennsylvania. Top of the Rock was the very first par-3 course to host a PGA championship, and it's easy to see why. (See page 80 for more of Missouri's top golf courses.)

4 Negro Leagues Baseball Museum

1616 E. 18th St., Kansas City, MO 64108; 816-221-1920
nlbm.com

The Negro Leagues Baseball Museum chronicles the history of segregated baseball and the athletes who played hard while also advancing the cause of social equality in the early 20th century. Exhibits begin with the founding of the original Negro National League in 1920, then run chronologically through the leagues which came after, up through 1962. Each era is well represented in this large space with a rich collection of memorabilia and thoroughly documented history, including Jackie Robinson breaking Major League Baseball's color barrier in 1947. One of the coolest parts of the museum is saved for last as visitors enter the Field of Legends, a mini baseball diamond populated by life-size bronze sculptures of league legends such as Josh Gibson, Cool Papa Bell, Buck O'Neil, Leroy "Satchel" Paige, and many others.

5 Bennett Spring State Park

26250 MO 64A, Lebanon, MO 65536; 417-532-4338
mostateparks.com/park/bennett-spring-state-park

If you're serious about trout fishing, then the cold, spring-fed waters of Bennett Spring State Park—arguably Missouri's best trout-fishing destination—are calling you. Opening day at the park is considered a holiday for many rural schools, with anglers converging from hundreds of miles around to claim their casting spots along the water. The spring provides 100 million gallons of cold, clean water each day, and the Missouri Department of Conservation stocks trout daily from its upstream hatchery operation. Get your tags at the park store, and sign up for lessons if you're new to the sport. When you've caught your limit, hatchery tours are also available, as are beautiful trails that meander throughout the park's 3,000-plus acres, including a natural tunnel featured in the Hiking section (see page 28).

6 World Chess Hall of Fame

4652 Maryland Ave., St. Louis, MO 63108; 314-367-9243
worldchesshof.org

For something more cerebral than sweaty, visit St. Louis's Central West End and the World Chess Hall of Fame, an impressive collection of chess history housed in a gorgeous historic building. It's easy to find, with the Guinness World Record–holding largest chess piece standing sentinel over the playable, oversize outdoor chessboard. Once inside, visitors enjoy a wealth of displays and artifacts from both the permanent collection and temporary exhibitions, all curated to highlight the legendary players, historic matches, and cultural relevance of chess throughout the ages. Everything from novelty and rare chess sets to fine art and important chess artifacts fills this bright space. The Saint Louis Chess Club is right across the street, along with a chess-themed diner guaranteeing an immersive day with no endgame in sight.

7 Wrestling at the South Broadway Athletic Club

2301 S. Seventh St., St. Louis, MO 63104; 314-776-4833; sbacstl.org

Twice a month, the South Broadway Athletic Club hosts one of the wildest, most intimate, and most unbelievably fun pro-wrestling shows anywhere. These aren't Olympic contests, but rather stylish choreographed brawls in the spirit of the WWE. For only a few bucks, patrons grab a seat in what feels like an odd, forgotten gymnasium where the energy of the crowd bounces off the walls, with cheers for the "faces" (good guys) and hissing for the "heels" (villains). The wrestlers, all local folks, put on a heck of a show for the crowd, with impressive aerial stunts and over-the-top drama including dirty refs. Matches are family friendly, but some colorful language is used, most often by the spectators, so don't be surprised. Reservations are recommended if you can't arrive early.

8 Missouri Sports Hall of Fame

3861 E. Stan Musial Drive, Springfield, MO 65809; 800-498-5678
mosportshalloffame.com

For sports fans not content to limit themselves to one particular team, the Missouri Sports Hall of Fame celebrates the greatness of all Missouri sports. From pro-sports legends to college dynasties and high school triumphs, every level of play is recognized here; every sport, too, with baseball, football, basketball, and much more. Even stock car racing and fishing make an appearance. There are a lot of fun interactive exhibits for the whole family, including shooting baskets, throwing a tight spiral, and driving your own (virtual) race car. The museum, a modest two floors but packed with memorabilia, also includes The Legends Walk of Fame, an outdoor stroll among busts and statues of the greatest figures in Missouri sports history.

9 Centene Community Ice Center

750 Casino Center Drive, Maryland Heights, MO 63043; 314-451-2244
centenecommunityicecenter.com

The official practice facility for Missouri's National Hockey League team, the St. Louis Blues, the Centene Community Ice Center is also a year-round community resource whose mission statement focuses on the idea that "hockey is for everyone!" To live up to that claim, the Centene houses four NHL-size rinks and offers space for all different types of ice sports, including free skating, figure skating, and public hockey sessions. As a full-service facility, they offer skate rentals and concessions, along with numerous classes for beginners or those looking to level up their skills. This is a busy facility, so check online or call ahead to make sure your preferred activity will be available when you arrive or to secure reservations for classes you're interested in.

Team Sports & Golf

Here's a quick rundown of Missouri's leading athletic teams, plus a list of the state's best golf courses.

Major League Teams

MAJOR LEAGUE BASEBALL

Kansas City Royals, Kauffman Stadium
1 Royal Way, Kansas City, MO 64129; 816-504-4040
mlb.com/royals/ballpark

St. Louis Cardinals, Busch Stadium
700 Clark Ave., St. Louis, MO 63102; 314-345-9600
mlb.com/cardinals/ballpark

NATIONAL FOOTBALL LEAGUE

Kansas City Chiefs, Arrowhead Stadium
1 Arrowhead Drive, Kansas City, MO 64129; 816-920-9300
chiefs.com

NATIONAL HOCKEY LEAGUE

St. Louis Blues, Enterprise Center
1401 Clark Ave., St. Louis, MO 63103; 314-622-5400
nhl.com/blues

MAJOR LEAGUE SOCCER

Sporting Kansas City, Children's Mercy Park
1 Sporting Way, Kansas City, KS 66111; 888-452-4625
sportingkc.com

St. Louis City SC
St. Louis's newest MLS team is scheduled to start playing in 2023.

NATIONAL WOMEN'S SOCCER LEAGUE

Kansas City
1800 Village West Pkwy, Kansas City, KS, 66111
www.kcwoso.com

Minor League Teams

ECHL (ICE HOCKEY)

Kansas City Mavericks, Cable Dahmer Arena
19100 E. Valley View Parkway, Independence, MO 64055; 816-442-6100
kcmavericks.com

MINOR LEAGUE BASEBALL

Springfield Cardinals (Double-A), Hammons Field
955 E. Trafficway St., Springfield, MO 65802; 417-863-0395
milb.com/springfield

MAJOR ARENA SOCCER LEAGUE

Kansas City Comets, Cable Dahmer Arena
19100 E. Valley View Parkway, Independence, MO 64055; 816-442-6100
kccomets.com

St. Louis Ambush, The Family Arena
2002 Arena Parkway, St. Charles, MO 63303; 636-896-4200
stlambush.com

NATIONAL PREMIER SOCCER LEAGUE

Club Atletico, St. Louis
4970 Oakland Ave., St. Louis, MO 63110; 314-531-0330
gobluebirds.com/home

Demize Soccer Academy, Cooper Sports Complex
2334 E. Pythian Drive, Springfield, MO 65802; 417-499-1459
demizesoccer.com/npsl-team

UNITED SOCCER LEAGUE

Sporting Kansas City II, Children's Mercy Park
1 Sporting Way, Kansas City, KS 66111; 888-452-4625
sportingkc.com/sportingkcii

St. Louis FC, West Community Stadium
1 Soccer Park Road, Fenton, MO 63026; 636-680-0997
saintlouisfc.com

St. Louis Lions, Tony Glavin Soccer Complex
2 Woodlands Parkway, Cottleville MO 63376; 636-939-5151
stllions.com

USA RUGBY

Kansas City Blues Rugby Club, Swope Soccer Village
6310 Lewis Road, Kansas City, MO 64132; 816-513-7500
kcblues.org

WORLD TEAM TENNIS

Springfield, Cooper Tennis Complex
2331 E. Pythian St., Springfield, MO 65802; 417-837-5800
springfieldlasers.com

NCAA Division I College Sports

Kansas City Roos (Basketball, Softball, Soccer)
University of Missouri–Kansas City, Kansas City; 816-235-2752
kcroos.com

Missouri State Bears (Football, Basketball, Baseball, Softball, Soccer)
Missouri State University, Springfield; 417-836-5402
missouristatebears.com

(continued on next page)

Mizzou Tigers (Football, Basketball, Baseball, Softball, Soccer)
University of Missouri, Columbia; 573-882-6501
mutigers.com

Saint Louis Billikens (Basketball, Baseball, Softball, Soccer)
Saint Louis University, St. Louis; 314-977-3462
slubillikens.com

Southeast Missouri State Redhawks (Football, Basketball, Baseball, Softball, Soccer)
Southeast Missouri State University, Cape Girardeau; 573-651-2113
gosoutheast.com

Golf

Bear Creek Valley Golf Club
910 MO 42, Osage Beach, MO 65065; 573-302-1000
bearcreekvalley.com

Buffalo Ridge Springs Golf Course
1001 Branson Creek Blvd., Hollister, MO 65672; 800-225-6343
bigcedar.com/golf/buffalo-ridge-springs-course

Branson Hills Golf Club
100 N. Payne Stewart Drive, Branson, MO 65616; 417-337-2963
bransonhillsgolfclub.com

Country Lake Golf Course
21309 Country Lakes Drive, Warrenton, MO 63383; 866-456-1165
countrylakegc.com

Eldon Golf Club
35 Golf Course Road, Eldon, MO 65026; 573-392-4172
eldongolfclub.com

The Golf Club at Deer Chase
770 Lowell Williams Road, Linn Creek, MO 65052; 866-633-3771
deerchasegolf.com

Innsbrook Resort Golf Course
1 Aspen Way Drive, Innsbrook, MO 63390; 636-928-3366, ext. 9203
innsbrook-resort.com/index.php/golf

Mozingo Lake Recreation Park Golf Course
1 Fall Drive, Maryville, MO 64468; 660-562-3864
mozingolake.com/golf

The Oaks at Margaritaville Lake Resort
494 Tan Tar A Drive, Osage Beach, MO 65065; 573-348-8522
margaritavilleresortlakeoftheozarks.com/play/golf/golf

Old Kinderhook Golf Course
678 Old Kinderhook Drive, Camdenton, MO 65020; 573-317-3500
oldkinderhook.com

Sports

The beauty of teeing up on a Missouri morning

Osage National Golf Resort
400 Osage Hills Road, Lake Ozark, MO 65049; 573-365-1950
osagenational.com

Redfield Golf and Country Club
14005 Redfield Drive, Eugene, MO 65032; 573-498-0110
redfieldgolf.com

Rolling Hills Country Club
13986 Country Club Road, Versailles, MO 65084; 573-378-5109
rollinghillsozark.com

Shoal Creek Golf Course
8905 NE Shoal Creek Parkway, Kansas City, MO 64157; 816-407-7242
shoalcreekgolf.com

Stone Canyon Golf Club
22415 E. 39th St., Blue Springs, MO 64015; 816-228-3333
stonecanyongolfclub.com

Sun Valley Golf Course
192 State Highway W, Elsberry, MO 63343; 573-898-2613
sunvalleygc.com

The magnificent Kansas Art Museum in Kansas City

THOUGH OFTEN REGARDED for its rural charm and natural beauty, Missouri is also home to significant centers of culture and cultivation. Dedication to the arts is evident in the world-class museums of St. Louis and Kansas City, but such appreciation also extends into galleries all across the state. This finely honed aesthetic extends into the horticultural world as well, with numerous gardening masterpieces that impress as much as any curated exhibition.

MUSEUMS, GARDENS & THE ARTS

(continued on next page)

Waterfall at the Missouri Botanical Gardens in St. Louis

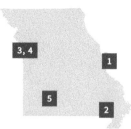

1 Saint Louis Art Museum

1 Fine Arts Drive, St. Louis, MO 63110; 314-721-0072
slam.org

Inside expansive Forest Park, you'll find one of the USA's premier art museums. However, unlike many across the country, the Saint Louis Art Museum is absolutely free, so you can come back as often as you like. Enter between the imposing columns, and prepare to be spoiled for choice with three full floors of paintings, sculpture, artifacts, and more from every corner of the globe. Permanent collections are dedicated to Asian, European, African, and Native American cultures, just to name a few, as well as robust temporary installations that cycle in and out over the year. There are works of ancient masters, masterpieces of fine art, boundary-pushing modern installations, and everything in between, including a unique offering: the Arms & Armor exhibit, a favorite of all ages.

2 Margaret Harwell Art Museum

421 N. Main St., Poplar Bluff, MO 63901; 573-686-8002
mham.org

Located inside a beautiful 19th-century home on the National Register of Historic Places, the Margaret Harwell Art Museum is an art lover's oasis in the Ozarks. The museum is named for a local business leader who left a portion of her estate to establish a center for the arts and to support the arts community in and around Poplar Bluff. It's a modestly sized museum, focused mainly on community-based art classes, juried competitions, and exhibitions, but is worth a look even if you're not a local to see the wonderfully preserved historic home, experience local art and artists, and check out the revolving special exhibitions featuring contemporary artists from all over the world. Free admission and a vibrant arts community await in this small country town.

3 The Nelson-Atkins Museum of Art

4525 Oak St., Kansas City, MO 64111; 816-751-1278
nelson-atkins.org

Standing like a fortress in the heart of Kansas City, the imposing façade of The Nelson-Atkins Museum of Art is nearly as grand as the artistic treasures contained within. Choose from any of several entrances in the original Nelson-Adkins building or the more modern Bloch Building addition. Once inside, enjoy world-class exhibits focusing on the work of African American artists, Chinese masters, centuries-old Japanese screens, a wide variety of South Asian and Southeast Asian works, ancient and contemporary Native American art and artifacts, architecture, photography, modern art, and more. There's also an extensive outdoor sculpture garden behind the main building and an enchanting Italian courtyard eatery. General admission is always free, but parking is not, so bring a few bucks in case the free spots along 45th Street and Rockhill Road are taken.

4 Kemper Museum of Contemporary Art

4420 Warwick Blvd., Kansas City, MO 64111; 816-753-5784
kemperart.org

The Kemper Museum of Contemporary Art is a sleek spaceship of futuristic architecture that mirrors the inspired collection of art found within. The museum contains both modern and contemporary art created over the past 100 years, including many artists still working today and in a variety of mediums. There are plenty of paintings, of course, but visitors will also find sculpture in classical style, photographs, films as well as provocative mixed-media amalgamations and sketches on paper. This is a great museum to bring your own sketchbook to so you can take a closer look at these modern masterpieces. The Kemper is also only a couple of blocks northwest of The Nelson-Adkins (see previous trip), so it's super easy to see both in one day. Admission is free as well as parking, though spaces are limited.

5 Springfield Art Museum

1111 E. Brookside Drive, Springfield, MO 65807; 417-837-5700
sgfmuseum.org

Located in Springfield's lovely Phelps Grove Park, the Springfield Art Museum is on the smaller side, but has a laid-back charm that makes each visit a real pleasure. The museum boasts a robust and rotating permanent collection focusing on American art, including an early Pollock, but also including art and artifacts from Europe, Asia, and around the world. Besides the exhibits, the Family Art Lab & Book Nook is a cool interactive space that makes this trip especially kid friendly. There are also frequent classes and workshops (sign up in advance) if you're

looking for something more immersive in your art outing. If, however, you just want to take your time, sit a spell, and let your mind wander, that is also encouraged here. Admission is free along with parking.

6 Pulitzer Arts Foundation

3716 Washington Blvd., St. Louis, MO 63108; 314-754-1850
pulitzerarts.org

For an artistic outing that is constantly evolving, look no further than the Pulitzer Arts Foundation in the heart of St. Louis. Describing itself as believing in "dynamic experiences with art," this mantra applies to the inspiring installations as well as the constantly changing exhibits on display. Unlike many museums, The Pulitzer has no major permanent collections, instead focusing on bringing in all-new exhibitions several times per year. Some are focused on a single artist, with others curated around a theme such as Japanese animation. Admission and parking are free, as is the case with most museums in St. Louis. But there are usually also several free events and programs happening at The Pulitzer as well, so it may be wise to check the website and plan ahead if you're interested in those.

7 Museum of Art and Archaeology & Museum of Anthropology

University of Missouri, 115 Business Loop 70 W., Columbia, MO 65211
Art and Archaeology: 573-882-3591, maa.missouri.edu
Anthropology: 573-882-3573, anthromuseum.missouri.edu

Part of the University of Missouri's flagship campus, these museums coexist in an oddly distant space from the rest of the college, at the almost eerily quiet Mizzou North building. As you enter, there is a small alcove to the right filled with classical statuary—a nice spot to sit and sketch if the mood strikes. Take the elevator up to the museums proper and pick whichever you'd like to visit first. Art and Archaeology covers fine art from ancient cultures up through the modern era, while Anthropology focuses on exhibiting items created for everyday use throughout history. There is some seeming overlap between the missions of the two museums, and both are fairly modest in size, but taken together they provide a thoroughly stimulating and insightful experience.

8 Powell Gardens

1609 NW US 50, Kingsville, MO 64061; 816-697-2600
powellgardens.org

Known as "Kansas City's Botanical Garden," Powell Gardens is actually more than 40 miles east of the city center, way out in the prairie fields of western Missouri, but with nearly 1,000 acres of rolling hills and lush landscaping, it's definitely worth the drive. Start at the bright, airy visitor center to buy tickets and get maps before venturing into the wide-open spaces beyond, where several themed garden spaces focus on different types of plants, including aquatic and woodland stream species, edible landscapes, perennials, and more. A favorite stop is the beautiful wooden chapel designed by a student of Frank Lloyd Wright. You're free to spend hours wandering at will, though there are usually programs and events happening from spring through fall that you can participate in as well.

Lily pad ponds at Powell Gardens

9 Missouri Botanical Garden

4344 Shaw Blvd., St. Louis, MO 63110; 314-577-5100
missouribotanicalgarden.org

In a city known for amazing greenspaces, the Missouri Botanical Garden is in a horticultural class by itself. Founded in the 19th century by local entrepreneur Henry Shaw, the garden is one of the oldest in the US and a National Historic Landmark. This pedigree is evident not only in the millions of meticulously landscaped specimens growing throughout the garden but also in the wealth of remarkable architecture found here. For a modest admission price, enjoy 97 plant-packed acres including the Japanese Garden, Shaw's Victorian home, the English-style Gladney Rose Garden, and the massive geodesic Climatron, which creates a mini rainforest in the Midwest. If you're bringing the kids, for an extra fee there's a 2-acre Children's Garden, which acts as a thrilling outdoor adventure park and educational experience in one.

One of many lovely scenes at the Missouri Botannical Garden

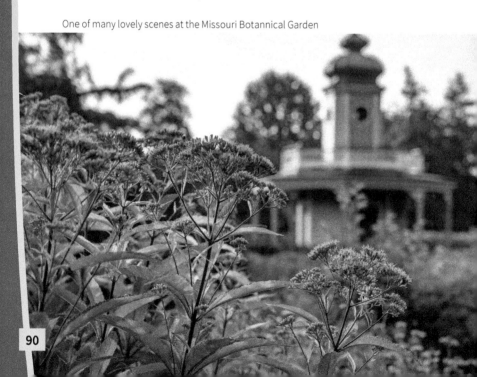

10 Shaw Nature Reserve

307 Pinetum Loop Road, Gray Summit, MO 63039; 314-577-9555
missouribotanicalgarden.org/visit/family-of-attractions/shaw-nature-reserve.aspx

An extension of the Missouri Botanical Garden, the Shaw Nature Reserve is the rambling country cousin of the family, covering 2,400 acres along the winding Meramec River. While managed intentionally for biological diversity and public education, the landscape evokes a sense of untouched natural wonder as it rolls across several distinct landscapes. There are quiet pine forests, swaying prairie grasses, wetlands, riverbanks, solitary lakes, and much more, all connected by a well-marked trail system. Several historic buildings also dot the grounds, providing some context for the spectacular natural world preserved here. There is an admission fee, but it's quite modest even compared with those of other gardens in the state, especially considering most visitors spend several hours exploring or just kicking back and taking it all in.

11 Springfield–Greene County Botanical Center

2400 S. Scenic Ave., Springfield, MO 65807; 417-891-1515
parkboard.org/274/springfield-botanical-gardens

Not as widely known as other botanical gardens in Missouri, the Springfield–Greene County Botanical Center is a hidden gem in the heart of the Ozarks. The Center covers 114 acres not far from downtown and focuses on cultivating a wealth of diverse flower species including hostas, daylilies, Asiatic lilies, iris, peonies, and roses, just to name a few. This makes the blooming seasons of late spring and summer are definitely the most beautiful times to visit. However, there are also other themed gardens that make for a lovely visit year-round. These include the Mizumoto Japanese Stroll Garden, with koi ponds, teahouse, and decorative bridges, and the Gray/Campbell Farmstead, boasting the oldest cabin in Springfield along with barns, a kitchen, a granary, an outhouse (for display only), and a one-room schoolhouse.

Peaceful downtown Rocheport

THE WORLD SEEMS intent on pushing us all closer and closer to the big cities, but Missouri maintains a fierce affection for the peace of small-town life just as it was here in generations past. Thankfully, this means that visitors still have quite a few options to choose from when they want to take things a little slower, or maybe even want to feel like they've stepped back in time.

SMALL-TOWN GETAWAYS

1 Weston

Chamber of Commerce: 526 Main St., Weston, MO 64098; 816-640-2909
westonmo.com

Just northwest of Kansas City is one of the most vibrant old small towns you'll find anywhere. Weston was an important port on the Missouri River during westward expansion and those riches built the fine architecture that lines main street. Nowadays, Weston is regularly voted "Best Day Trip" by several regional travel guides, and I'd have to agree. Local citizens and the chamber of commerce have built a robust, modern business district that thrives among these historic facades. Drive in to spend a day wandering from antiquery to art gallery, restaurant to coffee shop, or bike over on the lovely paved trail from Weston Bend State Park. The Chamber of Commerce also offers a self-guided driving tour that passes nearly a hundred antebellum houses, ancient mansions, and other historic places.

2 Cole Camp

Chamber of Commerce: PO Box 94, Cole Camp, MO 65325; 660-668-2295
colecampmo.com

Cole Camp is tucked away in a remote area of Missouri, far from any major population center, and is considered quaint even by the town's own residents. Its founding dates back to the early 1800s, and the residents' proud German heritage is apparent in many signs, storefronts, and celebrations to this day. In fact, the town is known in this rural area as a center for festivals, especially its Oktoberfest and the annual fair, which are some of the best times to visit. Besides festivals, there are a few interesting shops, a local history museum, and some savory restaurants to check out at any time of year. Pair a visit to Cole Camp with a jaunt over to nearby Warsaw on Lake of the Ozarks if you're looking for an even longer day of authentic small-town tranquility.

3 Hermann

Chamber of Commerce: 150 Market St., Hermann, MO 65041; 800-932-8687
visithermann.com

With its natural beauty, old-world charm, and all the wine you can drink, Hermann is considered one of the best getaways around. Founded by German settlers nostalgic for the homeland, it's chock-full of gorgeous old-world brick buildings, including more than 150 locations on the National Register of Historic Places. The rolling hills around the town, known as the Missouri Rhineland, support nearly a dozen local wineries, along with the city's wide variety of shops and restaurants and a thriving tourist economy. There's so much to do, you'll find something delightful around every corner. Be aware: Tuesday and Wednesday are the townsfolk's unofficial weekend, and most businesses are closed. Visitors can drive, bike in off the Katy Trail, or even catch a ride in on the Amtrak out of St. Louis.

4 Rocheport

School House Bed & Breakfast (official town representative), 504 Third St., Rocheport, MO 65279; 573-698-2022
rocheport.com

Tucked into a lovely hidden hollow on the banks of the Missouri River, Rocheport is an idyllic town with charm and natural beauty to spare. One of the big attractions here is the Katy Trail, so bring your bike if you can. The trail passes directly through town and offers easy access to the Katy's only train tunnel and a long stretch running alongside the high bluffs and roiling waters of the Missouri River. Another is Les Bourgeois Winery, a sprawling complex that sits on the bluffs overlooking the river and offers a variety of delicious ways to enjoy the view. The quiet, tree-lined streets also host a number of other restaurants, historic buildings, and shops selling antiques, fine art, and more. This is as peaceful as it gets.

5 Louisiana

Chamber of Commerce: 202 S. Third St., Ste. 207, Louisiana, MO 63353; 573-754-5921 or 636-891-5183
visitlouisianamo.com

If you're looking for a quiet day on the Mississippi River, it's hard to beat Louisiana, Missouri. While nearby Hannibal absorbs the Mark Twain tourist crowd, Louisiana offers a quieter retreat that's closer to what life would have been like all those years ago. The foremost attraction is the river itself, with amazing views from Riverfront and Riverview Parks and even the historic cemetery. This history is on full display in ornate downtown storefronts and the town's antebellum homes, including the highest concentration of Victorian architecture in the state. The Henry Lay Sculpture Park, a magnificent and bucolic sculpture garden just a few miles out of town, is a must-see as well. Besides taking in the views, check out the art, antiques, and local dining to round out your day.

Human hair art at Leila's Hair Museum

AS A GREAT AMERICAN CROSSROADS, Missouri has seen its share of strange events and eccentric visionaries who have decided to settle down and call this place home. These unique forces have left their mark on the state in ways that defy easy classification yet are undeniably compelling—easily worth a tank of gas to experience an unforgettable afternoon.

ODDS & ENDS

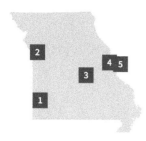

1 Red Oak II

12275 Kafir Road, Carthage, MO 64836; 417-237-0808
redoakiimissouri.com

On a lonely country road outside of Carthage sits one of the most color-ful and enchanting small towns anywhere. If you're lucky, you might even meet the town's founder, architect, mayor, and sole proprietor, Lowell Davis. Famous worldwide for figurines of bucolic rural scenes, Davis used his wealth to re-create his hometown of Red Oak from abandoned houses, gas stations, and even the general store he used to live in, moving dozens of whole buildings here while adding masterful sculptural flourishes as he went. Today, Davis can often be found sitting on his porch in outlaw Belle Starr's old house and greeting mesmerized visitors. After immersing yourself in this life-size art installation, drive back through Carthage, where you'll suddenly notice Lowell's inimi-table style in the signs of countless businesses throughout town.

2 Leila's Hair Museum

1333 S. Noland Road, Independence, MO 64055; 816-833-2955
leilashairmuseum.net

It's no stretch to say that this destination is one of a kind. Leila Cohoon is the proud owner of the world's only museum devoted to human hair. In the distant past, many families lacked easy access to supplies for making decorative items and artworks, but what they did have was an endless supply of their family's hair, which was woven into astonishingly intricate garlands, wreaths, jewelry, and much more. Leila has painstakingly curated this collection for more than 50 years, every wall and display case packed tight with this peculiar yet intriguing craftsmanship. Highlights include a mas-sive hair-art piece that was worked on continuously for more than 40 years; myriad styles of hair jewelry; and historical hair includ-ing locks from Queen Victoria, Abraham Lincoln, and even Ozzy Osbourne, who stopped in and left a few strands lighter.

3 Americana Antiques Tools & Books

1114 US 63 N., Vienna MO 65582; 573-422-3505
No website; look for the yellow eagle sign and red barn that says OLD BOOKS in big white letters.

Today, antiques shops are a dime a dozen, and too often an overpriced trudge through predictably curated aisles. However, Missouri boasts a destination that evokes awe and wonder in equal measure. Americana Antiques Tools & Books is a sprawling collection of surprises bursting out of several houses, barns, and cabins scattered across the landscape. Entering the main building feels like walking into a wizard's library with books packed, stacked, and arranged ceiling to floor and interspersed with photos, clothing, and countless artifacts from every conceivable niche of history. Because each building offers amazing browsing, multiple day trips are recommended. It can be difficult to find something specific, though thankfully the owner is more than glad to lead visitors around the property to whichever vault may have the treasure you're looking for.

4 Nuclear Waste Adventure Trail & Museum

7293 MO 94, St. Charles, MO 63304; 636-300-2601
energy.gov/lm/visit-weldon-spring-site-interpretive-center

At this eerie destination once stood a massive WWII-era explosives factory. During the Cold War, it transitioned to a nuclear-enrichment facility. But by the 1960s it was an abandoned, rotting shell of asbestos, corroding explosives, and radioactive waste. Today, after a herculean effort, this 45-acre site is home to an otherworldly-looking pyramid that rises 75 feet above the surrounding prairie and is engineered to safely contain this dangerous material for the next 1,000 years. It's worth the climb up its 75 stairs for the astounding view from the top of five surrounding counties and there is a nice little museum that details the history of the site. If you bring your bike, the 6-mile Hamburg Trail passes through connecting to the Katy Trail (see page 17) and a nearby conservation area.

5 Laclede's Landing Wax Museum

720 N. Second St., St. Louis, MO 63102; 314-241-1155
stlwaxmuseum.com

A kitschy mainstay of St. Louis culture since the 1980s, Laclede's Landing Wax Museum is an extensive collection of over 250 figures from real life and your most disturbing nightmares. The museum spreads its uncanny attractions over three floors and two basement levels in an old, labyrinthine building that leaves visitors feeling lost and disoriented but never bored. This is no prim and polished wax museum, instead embracing the dusty old building and the strangeness of it all. Figures themselves can often be difficult to identify, adding to the fun and humor of the experience as floors squeak and stairs creak around you. The basements are especially fun: They're literal horror shows with all manner of spooky and disturbing displays hidden among the gloom and damp stonework.

Odds & Ends

6 Precious Moments Chapel

4321 S. Chapel Road, Carthage, MO 64836; 800-543-7975
preciousmomentschapel.org

Depending on your age, and/or your relationship with your grandparents, your opinion of the Precious Moments Chapel may differ. Regardless, it's an essential experience that defies expectations. Built by Precious Moments creator Samuel Butcher, the "Chapel" consists of multiple buildings and extensive outdoor spaces, including the chapel, all dedicated to the artful realization of a world defined by impossibly large eyes and the gentle humanity behind them. Unironically referring to itself as "America's Sistine Chapel," the vast murals that cover the walls and striking sculptures that fill the grounds illustrate the intense religious faith that inspired the creation of the Precious Moments aesthetic. Whether you're visiting as a pious pilgrim or simply to marvel at the juxtaposition of the precious and the pious, this is a destination you'll tell stories about.

7 St. Joseph Museum Complex

3406 Frederick Ave., St. Joseph, MO 64506; 816-232-8471
stjosephmuseum.org

Admission to the complex grants you access to four different museums in this massive former hospital. These include a doll museum, the Black Archives Museum, and the Native American History Gallery. The primary draw for most visitors, however, is the Glore Psychiatric Museum, which spans four entire floors as it explores the history of psychiatric treatments, for better and, too often, for worse. The exhibits include devices that were used in what we now consider torture rather than treatment. There's a macabre humor at work in the exhibits as well: Check out the morgue in the basement for a recommended "selfie" opportunity, as well as the prescription-bottle mobile that hangs in the stairwell, and you may feel that something unsettling is still at work in these halls.

Electro Convulsive Therapy
St. Joseph State Hospital #2

Cannons stand sentinel at Wilson's Creek National Battlefield

DURING THE 19TH CENTURY, Missouri was considered the edge of the frontier. It was called the Gateway to the West; was home to the Pony Express; and, in many places, remained untouched by European expansion. As settlement increased, it also became the focus of over 1,000 battles during the Civil War. All these factors combined to create an indelible imprint of significant American history all over the state.

CIVIL WAR & THE WESTERN FRONTIER

1 Jesse James Farm and Museum

21216 Jesse James Farm Road, Kearney, MO 64060; 816-736-8500
jessejamesmuseum.org

Among Missouri's many famous outlaws, Jesse James stands tall as the most prodigious. A confederate guerrilla fighter in the Civil War, he later formed a gang and robbed trains and banks with a ruthless flair that turned him into a nationwide sensation. See where it all began at his birthplace, the Jesse James Farm and Museum, which is now owned and operated by Clay County as a tourist attraction and national landmark. Walk through the original James farmhouse and see the largest collection of James family artifacts anywhere. You can also wander the farm, including the banks of the little creek where Jesse and his brothers played as children, and see the original burial site of Jesse's body after his murder at the hands of Robert Ford.

2 Fort Osage National Historic Landmark

105 Osage St., Sibley, MO 64088; 816-650-3278
makeyourdayhere.com/205/fort-osage

Built in 1808 under the direction of William Clark (of Lewis & Clark fame), Fort Osage was constructed before the state of Missouri even existed, when all lands west of the Mississippi were merely part of the massive Louisiana Purchase frontier. The fort was later abandoned and by 1836 was stripped down to the stone foundation by scavenging settlers. However, in the 1940s, archaeologists rediscovered the forgotten site and, using Clark's original surveys, reconstructed the fort just as it would have stood more than 200 years ago. Now, Fort Osage is an impressive, fully immersive museum where historical interpreters in authentic period dress educate visitors about the daily life of military, civilian, and Native American peoples in and around the area. You'll also be able to take in the gorgeous views overlooking the Missouri River.

3 Wilson's Creek National Battlefield

6424 W. Farm Road 182, Republic, MO 65738; 417-732-2662, ext. 227
nps.gov/wicr

The first major Civil War battle west of the Mississippi River was fought at Wilson's Creek in southwest Missouri near Springfield.

Today, the history of that battle is preserved at the massive 1,700-plus-acre Wilson's Creek National Battlefield, operated by the National Park Service (NPS). As usual with NPS facilities, the grounds and historic structures are well kept, with plenty of interpretive signage about the battle. The visitor center also contains excellent exhibits, films, and interpreters on staff to help visitors get the best understanding of that bloody battle. There is also an extensive trail system in the park, perfect for a walk along picturesque Wilson's Creek itself and offering an opportunity to simply enjoy the landscape or to reflect on the conflicting nature of these peaceful fields and their tragic heritage.

4 Watkins Woolen Mill State Park and Historic Site

26600 Park Road N., Lawson, MO 64062; 816-580-3387
mostateparks.com/park/watkins-woolen-mill-state-historic-site

An invaluable look into Missouri's frontier past, Watkins Woolen Mill is a true living-history experience. Established in 1839, the small Watkins farm quickly grew into a highly diversified agricultural and industrial enterprise serving nearby settlers, as well as pioneers headed west, until the late 19th century, when mill operations ceased. Thanks to significant local and state-sponsored efforts, visitors today will discover the farm and mill in nearly the exact same condition as when it was in full operation. In fact, the mill itself is the only 19th-century textile mill in the United States with its original machinery intact. Also, as part of historic-preservation efforts by the state, the farm continues to raise heirloom vegetables as well as rare breeds of sheep and poultry on-site.

5 Smallin Civil War Cave

3575 N. Smallin Road, Ozark, MO 65721; 417-551-4545
smallincave.com

Smallin Civil War Cave is another of Missouri's beautiful underground galleries, featuring its share of impressive formations. However, this destination also boasts a significant historical record provided by early-19th-century geologist Henry Schoolcraft, who led one of the first European expeditions into the Ozark Mountains. He wrote extensively about Smallin Cave, then called Winoca by the Indigenous Osage who were still in the area. These writings became significant books on Ozark geology and are one of the main reasons this cave has the somewhat rare honor (for a cave) of being on the National Register of Historic Places. There is some evidence of Union soldier activity, but the more compelling artifacts are those of the native peoples, who carved petroglyphs and handholds into the formations. Available tours include conventional tours and "wild" tours that take you knee-deep into the frigid underground waters.

6 National Frontier Trails Museum

318 W. Pacific Ave., Independence, MO 64050; 816-325-7575
ci.independence.mo.us/nftm

During its time as the Gateway to the West, Missouri acted as a funnel through which pioneers passed as they loaded up with provisions, and the bustling town of Independence was considered the jumping-off point into their unknown futures. The National Frontier Trails Museum, an interpretive history museum and research library, chronicles many of the most famous westward routes, including the Oregon, Santa Fe, and California Trails, that originated here. Check out the films and exhibits, which provide an extensive history of the trails; then get hands-on with a covered wagon tour around historic Independence, and even touch history by walking among the wagon ruts created by thousands of migrant pioneers—so deep that they are still observable today—in a field directly across from the museum.

7 Battle of Island Mound State Historic Site

4837 NW County Road 1002, Butler, MO 64730; 417-276-4259
mostateparks.com/park/battle-island-mound-state-historic-site

The Battle of Island Mound took place in 1862 in the Kansas–Missouri border prairies. Considered a small-scale skirmish of the Civil War, it looms large in the American consciousness, as it was the first time a Black regiment appeared on the field of battle. Although significantly outnumbered by Confederate guerrilla fighters, the First Kansas Colored Infantry commandeered a local farm, which they named Fort Africa, and fought with what *The New York Times* called "desperate bravery," winning the battle decisively. This historic site has been preserved as a reminder of that bravery. Though the site consists of only a simple field with a small cabin and short interpretive trail, its remote, pastoral setting creates an atmosphere of peaceful reflection on the violent struggles that took place here not so long ago.

8 Missouri Civil War Museum

222 Worth Road, St. Louis, MO 63125; 314-845-1861
mcwm.org

As the third most contested state in the American Civil War, Missouri saw more than 1,000 battles on its soil between 1861 and 1865. So it's only fitting that the state is home to the Missouri Civil War Museum, which offers an incredibly comprehensive history of what happened in Missouri during those years. The museum houses thousands of artifacts, from weapons to uniforms to handwritten letters, that offer tangible insight into the lives of soldiers and civilians alike. Extensive historical context is offered at every turn, detailing Missouri's unique circumstances in the war, including how it came to have two functioning governments—one Union, another Confederate—operating at the same time. The museum sits next to the lovely Jefferson Barracks Park, which makes for a perfect walk to ponder what you just learned.

9 Patee House Museum and Jesse James Home

1201 S. 12th St., St. Joseph, MO 64503; 816-232-8206
ponyexpressjessejames.com

In the mid-1850s, the Patee House was built as a fabulous luxury hotel. Today, that grandeur houses the Patee House Museum, a highly entertaining destination that covers the local and national history of westward expansion. The museum focuses on transportation and even has a complete steam locomotive and a working carousel for those who like their trips to go around and around. The grounds are also the site of the original (relocated) home where Jesse James was murdered by Robert Ford. This is a worthy mini museum in its own right, with the infamous bullet hole still in the wall and an authentic casting of James's disinterred skull. The Patee House Museum keeps regular hours, but the James home is open only when a volunteer is available, so call ahead if you want to guarantee a visit.

10 Pony Express National Museum

914 Penn St., St. Joseph, MO 64503; 816-279-5059
ponyexpress.org

Although the Pony Express lasted only 18 months between 1860 and 1861, the romance and captivating stories surrounding these legendary rides made an indelible impact on the history of the West. As the eastern terminus for the Pony Express, St. Joseph features several commemorations of this service, the biggest and best being the Pony Express National Museum, housed in the original horse stables used by Express riders. There are exhibits dedicated to the more than 200 riders who worked for the Express, information on routes, and plenty of authentic artifacts that offer a complete accounting of this essential, if brief, effort. The museum is a worthwhile trip on its own, but it also pairs well with a visit to the Patee House Museum, a few blocks away.

Union Station in Kansas City

DARK HISTORY HIDES in the corners of small-town life and between the cracks of big-city bustle in every part of the world, and Missouri is no exception. Though known for their Show-Me State skepticism, many of its residents claim to have witnessed tragic and tortured ghosts reaching out across the veil. Here are some of Missouri's most frightening opportunities for your own ghostly encounter, along with some milder trips for those who like to keep the hereafter at a healthy distance.

HAUNTED MISSOURI

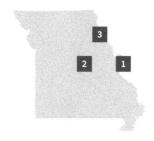

1 The Lemp Mansion

3322 DeMenil Place, St. Louis, MO 63118; 314-664-8024
lempmansion.com

The Lemp Mansion has been included in top-10 lists such as America's Most Haunted Houses and World's Spookiest Buildings and has been featured on *Ghost Hunters,* where it was declared "definitely haunted." Such a paranormal pedigree makes this a must-visit destination for any supernatural enthusiast. Once the site of one of America's biggest breweries, the mansion and caves beneath are said to be haunted by generations of the aristocratic Lemp family, whose scandals and suicides have created unearthly attachments that manifest themselves to visitors in a variety of unnerving ways. The current caretakers offer Haunted History Tours, the Lemp Mansion Experience (a dark tour with infrared cameras), and even overnight stays at the on-site bed-and-breakfast. Reservations are required, so be sure to call ahead.

2 Missouri State Penitentiary

115 Lafayette St., Jefferson City, MO 65101; 866-998-6998
missouripentours.com

Opened in 1836 and in continuous operation until 2004, the grounds of the Missouri State Penitentiary have witnessed human tragedy on a massive scale for nearly two centuries. Inside its sprawling Gothic architecture, visitors can enjoy tours focused on history and photography. But for those looking for something more spine-tingling, choose one of a wide variety of paranormal tours, including ghost tours, ghost hunts, ghost-hunting classes, and even extensive overnight investigations that will test the stamina of even the nervi-est supernatural sleuth. Knowledgeable guides lead tour groups through the cold stone and damp tunnels of what *Time* magazine once dubbed "the 47 bloodiest acres in America." Reservations are required, so book ahead. Also, due to the violent subject matter and overall fright factor, all ghost tours have firm minimum age requirements of 14 or even 18 to participate.

3 Haunted Hannibal Ghost Tours

200 N. Main St., Hannibal, MO 63401; 573-248-1819
hauntedhannibal.com

Cell block at Missouri State Penitentiary

Tourism in Hannibal, Missouri's official Mark Twain city, often focuses on the author's life and the old-timey era of his work. However, around dusk there's an opportunity to see the shadowy side of this charming river village. Ghost tours are shuttle-based and carry visitors to the most haunted locations in Hannibal, while guides offer a thorough history of the murders and mystery that lurk along downtown streets and the mansions of Millionaire's Row. A special treat is the stop at the Old Baptist Cemetery, where visitors disembark to investigate graves dating back to the Civil War and try their hand at using dowsing rods to detect nearby spectral activity. Dark in subject matter but not overly scary, this tour is appropriate for almost any audience.

4 Pythian Castle

1451 E. Pythian St., Springfield, MO 65802; 417-865-1464
pythiancastle.com

The magnificent Pythian Castle looks like something out of a fairy tale, but this charming façade is not all it appears to be. The castle was built in 1913 by the fraternal order of the Knights of Pythias to serve as an orphanage and was appropriated by the military during World War II to function as a rehab center, tuberculosis ward, and POW camp for wounded soldiers from both sides. With such a pedigree, the site is well documented; at least 100 deaths have occurred on-site over the years, and numerous eerie first-hand encounters with those lingering spirits have been reported. The castle has even received "certified haunted" designation from TV shows such as *Ghost Adventures, Ghost Lab,* and *Haunted Collector.* Today, visitors can book evening ghost tours or extensive overnight ghost investigations hosted by Missouri's own Paranormal Task Force.

5 Belvoir Winery

1325 Odd Fellows Road, Liberty, MO 64068; 816-200-1811
belvoirwinery.com

Operated primarily as a winery and extravagant events venue, the manicured magnificence of the Belvoir Winery also plays host to the spirits of some 10,000 souls that have perished here since the early 1900s. Originally constructed as an asylum by the Independent Order of Oddfellows, the site consists of four buildings that were used as a hospital, an orphanage, an old folks home, and even a morgue. Today, the winery is housed primarily in the gorgeous architecture of the renovated orphanage, while the other grand buildings remain in various states of disrepair, all of them hot spots for paranormal encounters. The focus of episodes of *Ghost Hunters* and *Ghost Adventures,* the winery offers tours led by the Paranormal Research Investigators; book yours by calling ahead or clicking on the Public Events page of Belvoir's website.

6 Zombie Road in Wildwood

Rock Hollow Trail; 777 Ridge Road, Ellisville, MO 63021 (trailhead); 314-436-7009
alltrails.com/trail/us/missouri/rock-hollow-trail

Originally called Lawler Ford Road and built in the 1860s, this 2-plus-mile path is a legend among local thrill-seekers who recount run-ins with spectral Native Americans from a nearby burial mound, see-through Confederate soldiers, child ghosts, and shadow men who stalk the hills. In 2010, the Great Rivers Greenway turned Lawler Ford into a paved multiuse path called the Rock Hollow Trail, which has somewhat dampened the mystique; however, stories of terrifying encounters continue. The trailhead is most easily accessed from the parking lot of Ridge Meadows Elementary School, but avoid going in the evening: Zombie Road is now under the jurisdiction of local police, who strictly enforce local ordinances by writing expensive tickets for anyone caught out on the trail more than half an hour after sunset without permission.

7 Union Station in Kansas City

30 W. Pershing Road, Kansas City, MO 64108; 816-460-2020
unionstation.org

One of the more low-key haunted locations in Missouri, Kansas City's Union Station is known primarily for its highly decorative Beaux Arts–style architecture and is considered a must-see landmark. However, a consistent history of spectral encounters here has also earned it a reputation as one of the state's most haunted places. Visitors and staff have reported sightings of a woman in black and another in white who seem to walk briskly toward the train platforms only to disappear if approached. Another phantom is that of the gangster Frank "Jelly" Nash, who was gunned down here in the headline-making Kansas City Massacre. There are no official ghost tours at the station, but a late-night outing to take in the grand setting is also an opportunity to catch a glimpse of a less tangible past.

8 The Paranormal Path

Independence, MO (multiple locations)
visitindependence.com/paranormal-path

A bit of clever branding from the local Chamber of Commerce, The Paranormal Path is nonetheless a fascinating trio of haunted locations with all the macabre history a ghost hunter could ask for. The first stop is often the Vaile Mansion, whose matriarch died of an overdose and which was later converted to a primitive sanitorium where patients are said to have been tortured, sometimes to death. Next, visit the 1859 Jail, where visitors have reported odd feelings of cold and nausea along with hearing the disembodied growls of men who aren't there. If you're still feeling brave, finish up at the Bingham-Waggoner Estate, which marks the starting point for the Santa Fe Trail and is home to a mysterious woman in white who died here on her wedding day. Tours for each location can be booked directly on the website.

9 St. Charles Ghost Tour

101 S. Main St., St. Charles, MO 63301 (tour meets outside); 314-374-6102
stcharlesghosts.com

Don't expect to encounter any lonely phantoms on this spirited walking tour in the heart of downtown; it's usually a little too bustling for that. But do expect to hear a fascinating and spooky history of the area while accompanied by your jovial and knowledgeable guide, who literally wrote the book on St. Charles's ghosts. Tales of a dead sheriff, the tragic demise of a young mother, a lost graveyard, and the roaming ghosts of Lewis and Clark's dogs are just a few of the tales that haunt these streets and alleys, all only steps away from the banks of the Missouri River. It's hard to beat the charm and ambience of this outdoor outing when the weather is nice. Tours fill up fast, so plan well ahead and make a reservation.

10 STL Haunted History

721 N. Second St., St. Louis, MO 63102 (tours begin at Morgan Street Brewery); 314-800-6369; stlhauntedhistory.com

St. Louis was founded before the Declaration of Independence and has acted as a major center of commerce and cultural crossroads ever since. As such, the city is rich in history, for better or worse. For those with a keen interest in the "worse," STL Haunted History walking tours are one of the best ways to get acquainted with the tragic tales and haunted happenings in the Gateway City. Tour topics include The Great St. Louis Fire and cholera epidemic of 1849, the actual exorcism from *The Exorcist,* the pistol duels of Bloody Island, and much more. These chilling and fascinating tales are related to each group against the backdrop of historic Laclede's Landing by talented storyteller David Riordan, who clearly enjoys his work and whose family has lived in St. Louis for generations.

11 The Joplin Spook Light

West on E 50 Road off State Line Road just inside the Oklahoma border
joplinmo.org/575/the-spook-light

The Joplin Spook Light (aka the Ozark Spook Light, the Hornet Ghost Light, and the Tri-State Spook Light) is a bright, ghostly orb that has appeared on a lonely country road near the Missouri–Oklahoma border for more than 100 years. Self-appointed experts have claimed to debunk the phenomenon, only for others to debunk the debunkers, while the light continues to float on through the generations, just out of reach. Why not decide for yourself whether this spectral light show is a real will-o-the-wisp or not? To reach the Spook Light, travel southwest of Joplin and follow State Line Road (also called S 700 Road) south until the junction with E 50 Road. Turn west on E 50 and travel to a dip in the road, about 2 miles down, to find the darkest and best place to park and wait.

The quaint streets of old St. Charles

Wine with a river view at Les Bourgeois

FRUIT OF THE BRANCH & VINE

WINERIES

Adam Puchta Winery
1947 Frene Creek Road, Hermann, MO 65041; 573-486-5596
adampuchtawine.com

Augusta Winery
5601 High St., Augusta, MO 63332; 888-667-9463
augustawinery.com

Belvoir Winery
1325 Odd Fellows Road, Liberty, MO 64068; 816-200-1811
belvoirwinery.com

Black River Wine House
50129 MO 49, Annapolis, MO 63620; 314-550-5422
blackriverwinehouse.com

Cave Vineyard, Winery & Distillery
21124 Cave Road, Ste. Geneviève, MO 63670; 573-543-5284
cavevineyard.com

Cedar Lake Cellars
11008 Schreckengast Road, Wright City, MO 63390; 636-745-9500
cedarlakecellars.com

Chandler Hill Vineyard
596 Defiance Road, Defiance, MO 63341; 636-798-2675
chandlerhillvineyards.com

Chaumette Vineyards & Winery
24345 State Highway WW, Ste. Geneviève, MO 63670; 573-747-1000
chaumette.com

Dale Hollow Winery
314 E. First St., Stover, MO 65078; 573-569-0094
dalehollowwinery.com

(continued on next page)

Four Horses and a Dog Winery
15010 Salem Road, Excelsior Springs, MO 64024; 816-582-4648
fourhorsesandadogwinery.com

Hermannhof Winery
330 E. First St., Hermann, MO 65041; 800-393-0100
hermannhof.com

Jowler Creek Vineyard & Winery
16905 Jowler Creek Road, Platte City, MO 64079; 816-858-5528
jowlercreek.com

Keltoi Winery
17705 County Road 260, Oronogo, MO 64855; 417-642-6190
keltoivineyard.com

Le Bourgeois Vineyards
14020 W. State Highway BB, Rocheport, MO 65279; 800-690-1830
missouriwine.com

Montelle Winery
201 Montelle Drive, Augusta, MO 63332; 888-595-9463
montelle.com

Pirtle Winery
502 Spring St., Weston, MO 64098; 816-640-5728
pirtlewinery.com

Red Moose Vineyard
425 State Highway VV, Salem, MO 65560; 573-743-3006
redmoosevineyard.com

Röbller Vineyard
275 Röbller Vineyard Road, New Haven, MO 63068; 573-237-3986
robllerwines.com

Seven Springs Winery
846 Winery Hills Estate, Linn Creek, MO 65052; 573-317-0100
sevenspringswinery.com

Shawnee Bluff Winery
2430 Bagnell Dam Blvd., Lake Ozark, MO 65049; 573-365-9935
shawneebluff.com

St. James Winery
540 State Highway B, St. James, MO 65559; 800-280-9463
stjameswinery.com

Stone Hill Winery
1110 Stone Hill Highway, Hermann, MO 65041; 573-486-2221
stonehillwinery.com

Villa Antonio Winery
3660 Linhorst Road, Hillsboro, MO 63050; 636-475-5008
villaantoniowinery.com

ORCHARDS & BERRY PICKING

Alldredge Orchards
10455 State Highway N, Platte City, MO 64079; 816-330-3448
alldredgeorchards.com

Brown's Berry Farm
5935 State Highway M, Miller, MO 65707; 417-452-2400
facebook.com/brownsberryfarmmillermo

Buckeye Acres Produce
91 NE 600th Road, Warrensburg, MO 64093; 660-747-7760
buckeye-acres.com

Centennial Farms and Orchard
199 Jackson St., Augusta, MO 63332; 636-228-4338
centennialfarms.biz

Crafty Farms
30558 US 60, Pierce City, MO 65723; 417-669-7792
facebook.com/craftyfarmsupick

(continued on next page)

Missouri is an apple picker's paradise

Sunset over historic Hermann

Fahrmeier Farm
9133 County Farm Road, Lexington, MO 64067; 816-888-9490
ourfamilyfarmer.com

Herman's Farm Orchard
3663 N. MO 94, St. Charles, MO 63301; 636-925-9969
hermansfarm.weebly.com

Historic Weston Orchard & Vineyard
18545 County Road H, Weston, MO 64098; 816-253-8240
orchardweston.com

Hunter's Ridge Berry Farm
3757 Sunny Road, Washington, MO 63090; 314-808-6386
facebook.com/huntersridgeberryfarm

John & Linda's U-Pick Fruit and Berry Farm
2428 Texas Prairie Road, Bates City, MO 64011; 816-690-6293
tinyurl.com/johnandlindasupick

Lost Branch Blueberry Farm
21507 Lost Branch Way, Brashear, MO 63533; 660-342-2725
lostbranchblueberries.com

Schweizer Orchards
5455 SE State Highway FF, St. Joseph, MO 64507; 816-232-3999
schweizerorchards.com

Sunshine Valley Farm
8011 E. State Highway AD, Rogersville, MO 65742; 417-753-2698
sunshinevalleyfarm.com

Thierbach Orchards & Berry Farm
85 Town Branch Road (Berry and Peach Orchard), 18427 MO 47 (Apple Orchard), Marthasville, MO 63357; 636-433-2299
thierbachorchards.com

West Orchards
25875 Jewell Ave., Macon, MO 63552; 660-651-7582
west-orchards.com

Wind Ridge Farm
3511 State Highway F, New Melle, MO 63365; 636-828-5900
windridgefarm.net

Treasures piled high at a Missouri Antique Mall

ANTIQUES & FLEA MARKETS

ANTIQUES

Annie Laurie's
536 Broadway, Cape Girardeau, MO 63701; 573-339-1301
annielauries.net

Apple Tree Mall
1830 W. 76 Country Blvd., Branson, MO 65616; 417-335-2133
tiny.one/appletreemall

Aunt Polly's Treasures
213 Hill St., Hannibal, MO 63401; 573-221-1496
auntpollystreasures.com

The Brass Armadillo
1450 Golfview Drive, Grain Valley, MO 64029; 888-847-5260
brassarmadillo.com/kansascity

Camp Flea Antique Mall
1900 W. Elm St., Ozark, MO 65721; 417-581-2575
campflea.com

Downtown Antiques
1 Court Square, West Plains, MO 65775; 417-256-6487
dtantiques.com

Fox and Hound Antiques
625 S. Main St., St. Charles, MO 63301; 314-660-2847 (call before visiting)
facebook.com/foxandhoundantiques625

Good Time Antiques
121 W. Davis St., Mound City, MO 64470; 660-442-3337
facebook.com/rasnicsgoodtimeantiques

(continued on next page)

A bustling flea market

Hermann's Attic Antique Mall
220 E. First St., Hermann, MO 65041; 573-486-9121
hermannsattic.com

Old Village Mercantile
219 S. MO 21, Caledonia, MO 63631; 573-779-3907
oldvillagemercantile.com

Pastimes Antiques
45 Main St., Cape Girardeau, MO 63701; 573-332-8882
pastimesantiques.com

Patricia's Victorian House
101 W. Main St., Branson, MO 65616; 417-335-8000
facebook.com/victorianhousebranson

Rangeline Antique Mall
3421 N. Rangeline Road, Joplin, MO 64801; 417-782-7505
rangelineantiquemall.com

Relics Antique Mall
2015 Battlefield Road, Springfield, MO 65807; 417-885-0007
relicsantiquemall.com

River Market Antiques
115 W. Fifth St., Kansas City, MO 64105; 816-221-0220
rivermarketantiquemall.com

FLEA MARKETS

F & L Flea Market
119 N. Allen St., Centralia, MO 65240; 573-228-0012
facebook.com/f-and-l-fleamarket-157825534278880

Fancy Flamingo Flea Market
5171 N. Main St., Joplin, MO 64801; 417-553-8142
facebook.com/fancyflamingofleamarket

Grand Slam Market Place
10041 Lewis and Clark Blvd., St. Louis, MO 63136; 314-246-9918
grandslamstoragecenter.com/self-storage/mo/st-louis/lewis-clark-blvd

Itchy's Flea Market
1907 Providence Road, Columbia, MO 65202; 573-443-8275
sites.google.com/a/hauptmanns.com/itchys

Nate's Swap Shop (63rd Street Drive-In)
8200 E. 63rd St., Kansas City, MO 64133; 816-353-1627
natesswapshop.com

The Old Time Flea Market
4335 Showplace Drive, Farmington, MO 63640; 573-747-0003
theoldtimefleamarket.com

Rutledge Flea Market
State Highway V, Rutledge, MO 63563; 660-216-3223
facebook.com/rutledgefleamarket

Super Flea
6200 St. John Ave., Kansas City, MO 64123; 816-241-5049
facebook.com/superfleakc

Wentzville Community Club Flea Market
500 W. Main St., Wentzville, MO 63385; 636-357-4328
wentzvillecommunityclub.com/flea-market

Missouri State Capitol, Jefferson City

MISSOURI STATE
Symbols, Emblems, & Trivia

COUNTIES: 114* *Note:* St. Louis is an independent city and doesn't belong to a county.
POPULATION, PER THE US CENSUS: 6,137,428
FOUNDING AS US STATE: August 10, 1821 *(24th state to enter the Union)*

STATE FLAG

Missouri joined the Union in 1821, relatively early in the country's history, but it didn't have an official flag until 1913, when a flag was proposed by Mrs. Marie Elizabeth Oliver. The state coat of arms is at the center of the flag. It features 24 stars, one for each state of the Union, a pair of grizzly bears, symbolizing Missouri's size and strength, and two mottos: "United We Stand, Divided We Fall" and *Salus Populi Suprema Lex Esto*, a Latin saying made famous by Cicero, which translates to "Let the good of the people be the supreme law." Oddly, grizzly bears, unlike black bears, aren't native to the state.

STATE FLOWER: Hawthorn Blossom
(Crataegus spp.)

Famous for their beautiful white flowers in spring and their bright red crabapple-like fruits that persist through fall, hawthorn flowers are the state flower of Missouri. Dubbed the official bloom in 1923, the original legislation didn't name a particular species as the "official" flower, just the genus *Crataegus*. As there are 70-some species of hawthorns found in Missouri, this leads to some confusion, but all hawthorns are large shrubs or small trees, bear "haws" (berries), and many also have thorns, giving them their common name.

STATE TREE: Flowering Dogwood *(Cornus florida)*

Blooming in April to May, the Flowering Dogwood is perhaps best described as a tree-like shrub or a shrubby tree. Either way, it's not a towering plant, but when it comes to visual appeal, it's simply gorgeous, as each plant practically bursts forth with many bracts (petal-like structures). One tree by itself is gorgeous, but when seen en masse and with the Ozarks as a backdrop, it's really an experience.

STATE FISH: Channel Catfish *(Ictalurus punctatus)*

Missouri is home to more than 100,000 miles of streams and rivers, and not suprisingly, it's also known for its fishing. Catfish, in particular, are a major draw for some anglers. (In fact, a 130-pound former world record catfish was caught in Missouri in 2010; that record has since been eclipsed.) The Channel Catfish, which became the state fish in 1997, doesn't reach the same size as its Blue Catfish cousins, but it is found throughout the state, and it's fairly easy to catch. In addition to traditional baits such as worms and minnows, catfish anglers have found success with everything from deli meat to soap. (Catfish can see fairly well, but their sense of smell is incredibly acute. This can make "stink bait" effective when targeting them.)

STATE BIRD: Eastern Bluebird *(Sialia sialis)*

The Eastern Bluebird has been Missouri's state bird since 1927, and it's an apt choice. Bluebirds are common throughout the state and easy to attract, either by putting out an artificial nest box or by feeding them a dish of wiggly mealworms. (They don't come to seed feeders.) The bright blue males, and the more subdued, but equally gorgeous females, live year-round in many parts of Missouri.

STATE MINERAL AND STATE ROCK:
Galena and Mozarkite

Missouri's state mineral is galena, which also the primary source of the metal lead. Historically, Missouri was home to several lead districts, and it's still dealing with a

Galena

Mozarkite

legacy of lead pollution and high levels of lead poisoning today. As a mineral, galena is beautiful and safe to collect (as long as you don't contact it for long and wash your hands afterward).

Mozarkite, Missouri's state rock, is a beautiful variety of chert. Its name is a combination of the abbreviation for Missouri (MO), and a nod to the Ozarks (zark). It's mostly found in west-central Missouri.

STATE INSECT: Honeybee *(Apis mellifera)*

Honeybees might seem like a bit of an odd choice for Missouri's state insect, given that they are an introduced species. Originally found in Europe, Africa, and the Middle East, the honeybee has been intro-

duced worldwide. Today honeybees are an essential component of agriculture, as they help pollinate a huge variety of crops in Missouri, including watermelons, grapes, apples, and more.

Farmers purchase honeybees (and sometimes bumblebees) and then set their hives near the crops to be pollinated. The bees then do what they do best: visit flowers, gather nectar and pollen, and pollinate plants.

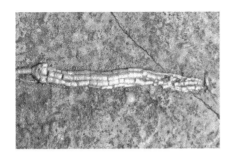

STATE FOSSIL: Crinoid
(Delocrinus missouriensis)

Relatives of starfish that lived 300 million years ago, crinoids once lived in an ancient sea that once covered much of Missouri. Crinoids still exist in oceans today, though they are much rarer than they once were. If you've ever seen a crinoid in real life you can see why they get the name "sea lilies." These filter-feeders are perched upon a stem and have showy, often colorful, feather-like rays that they use to capture food. Crinoids among the more common fossils one will find in MIssouri (and in many places of the Midwest), but most crinoid finds consist of bits and pieces of the stems; these look a little bit like Cheerios and can be found in large numbers. Missouri's official state crinoid is *Delocrinus missouriensis*, but many other varieties are found in the state as well.

STATE AMPHIBIAN: American Bullfrog *(Rana catesbeiana)*

It's hard to tell whether the American Bullfrog gets its name from its size—some can reach more than two pounds—or its deep cow-like call, but either way, this is one impressive frog. Found throughout Missouri, bullfrogs are largely aquatic, and they eat just about anything from bugs to small birds. In turn, some people eat bullfrog legs; in fact, in Missouri, bullfrogs are classified as a game animal and there is a specific season for harvesting them.

STATE ANIMAL:
Missouri Mule

Missouri's long agricultural history led to the mule being dubbed the state's official animal in 1995. Mules are hybrid animals that are produced when a female horse and a male donkey reproduce. This "best of both worlds" approach gives mules the strength of a horse, and the stubborn work ethic of a donkey. After they were introduced to Missouri in the early 1800s, mules became highly sought after by farmers and settlers and they remained a farmyard necessity until the adoption of the tractor in the 1940s.

STATE AQUATIC ANIMAL: Paddlefish
(Polyodon spathula)

At first glance, spotting a paddlefish while floating down a river might give you a bit of a scare: they have a shark-like tail, can reach huge sizes—Missouri is home to the world-record fish of 140 lb., 9 oz.—and they have a long, paddle-like snout. Often described as a "living fossil" because they've existed relatively unchanged since the Cretaceous period (65 million years ago), paddlefish are actually filter-feeders, entirely harmless, and can reach up to 50 years in age. The American Paddlefish is actually the only remaining paddlefish species; a related species, the Chinese Paddlefish was recently declared extinct. American Paddlefish numbers have declined as well, but Missouri's population is sustained by hatchery-produced fish.

STATE REPTILE:
Three-Toed Box Turtle
(Terrapene carolina triunguis)

The Three-Toed Box Turtle embodies the popular trope of the slow-moving but persistent turtle that is found in everything from cartoons to children's books. Unlike most of Missouri's other turtles, the Three-Toed Box Turtle lives exclusively on land. It's found in forests and prairies. In spring, males often set out to find their own territory; unfortunately, the combination of their slow speed, and their preference for warm, wide-open spaces (including roads), makes them especially susceptible to vehicle traffic. If you spot one trying to cross the road, move it to the other side of the road if traffic conditions safely allow it!

STATE INVERTEBRATE:
Crayfish

A familiar crustacean across Missouri, crayfish are common in Missouri. Around 30 species are found in the state, and they are an important food source for game fish and a popular fish bait. And in the Ozarks, crayfish boils are a popular (and tasty) pasttime as well.

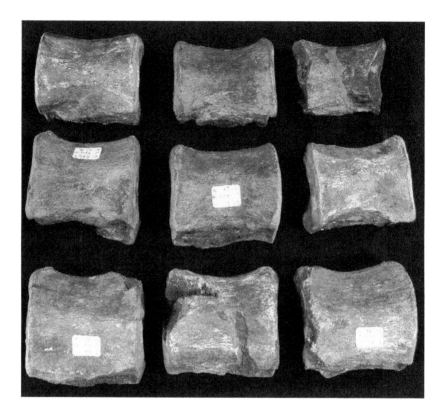

STATE DINOSAUR: Hadrosaur *(Hypsibema missouriensis)*

Commonly known as duck-billed dinosaurs, Hadrosaurs were large plant-eating dinosaurs famous for their "duck-like" bills, which they used to chomp on tough, low-growing plants. A hadrosaur fossil was discovered in Missouri in 1942 when the Chronister family was digging a well; in a happy coincidence, Dan Stewart, a staff member of the Missouri Geological Survey encountered an eight-year-old member of the family, Ole, who mentioned the bones his family had found. Stewart examined them and knew that they were dinosaur bones, and eventually the family sold them to the Smithsonian for $50. The hadrosaur became the official dinosaur of Missouri in 2004. The original bones (vertebrae) are shown above and are still housed at the Smithsonian.

The ice cream cone, Missouri's state dessert since 2008, was invented in St. Louis at the 1904 World's Fair

Index

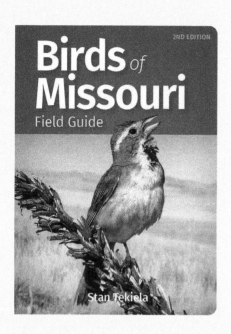

LEARN TO IDENTIFY BIRDS IN MISSOURI!

Birds of Missouri Field Guide

Stan Tekiela

ISBN: 978-1-64755-085-1 • $14.95 • 4.38 x 6 • paperback
324 pages • full-color photos

Make bird-watching even more enjoyable! With Stan Tekiela's famous field guide, bird identification is simple and informative. There's no need to look through dozens of photos of birds that don't live in your area. This book features 124 species of Missouri birds, organized by color for ease of use. Do you see a yellow bird and don't know what it is? Go to the yellow section to find out. Fact-filled information, a compare feature, range maps, and detailed photographs help to ensure that you positively identify the birds that you see.

EXPLORE THE REGION'S BEST TRAILS!

Five-Star Trails: The Ozarks

Jim Warnock

**ISBN: 978-1-6340-401-5 • $15.95 • 5 x 8
paperback • 278 pages**

The Ozark Mountain region offers some of the country's most beautiful and diverse landscapes. The Mark Twain National Forest in Missouri is home to pristine natural springs. The Ozark National Forest in Arkansas provides a rugged mountain canvas, and the Arkansas River Valley features the towering Cedar Falls. Hiking expert and Ozarks native Jim Warnock shares everything you need to know about 43 five-star hiking trails. Every trail is rated for scenery, difficulty, trail condition, solitude, and accessibility for children, so you'll know exactly what to expect on your next adventure.

About the Author

Brian Blair grew up on a small family farm in the Missouri Ozarks, where he developed a deep appreciation for the people and landscape of his home state. For the past 20 years, he has lived and worked all over the United States. He has wrangled giraffes and rhinos in the Louisiana bayou and bear dogs in the mountains of Montana, and he's worked to preserve hellbender habitat in Appalachian Ohio. He recently completed his MFA in fiction at the University of Missouri and is on the road again in a beat-up old RV with his wife, daughter, and Great Pyrenees, collecting stories for his first novel.

CPSIA information can be obtained
at www.ICGtesting.com
Printed in the USA
JSHW011059060621
15357JS00003B/1